Understanding the Multi-Problem Family:

A CONCEPTUAL ANALYSIS AND

EXPLORATION IN EARLY IDENTIFICATION

Understanding the

Multi-Problem Family:

L. L. Geismar

and Michael A. La Sorte

A CONCEPTUAL ANALYSIS

AND EXPLORATION IN

EARLY IDENTIFICATION

ASSOCIATION PRESS · NEW YORK

301.42
G 27 u

UNDERSTANDING THE MULTI-PROBLEM FAMILY

Copyright © 1964 by
National Board of Young Men's Christian Associations

Association Press, 291 Broadway, New York, N.Y. 10007

50190
July 1965

Publisher's stock number: 1546
Library of Congress catalog card number: 64-12029

Printed in the United States of America

ACKNOWLEDGMENTS

A good number of people have directly or indirectly contributed to this book. Alice Overton's leadership in the Family Centered Project of St. Paul, Minnesota, ensured a setting in which conceptual thinking and research could become partners to practice, in the work with the multi-problem family. The untiring efforts of Frank Harris resulted in the Neighborhood Improvement Project of New Haven, Connecticut, where ideas and methods developed in St. Paul could be tested further. We are particularly indebted to the director of the New Haven project, Jane Krisberg, for assistance and collaboration in developing a research program which included the early identification study reported here. The work of Beverly Ayres at the St. Paul Family Centered Project has played a key role in the development of research techniques used in the present volume. The joint surveys by Dr. Joseph Lagey and Beverly Ayres in Vancouver, B.C., on multi-problem family projects in North America have supplied basic information for the last chapter of this book.

We gratefully acknowledge the contribution of the treatment staff and the research interviewers who gathered data for the early identification study in the New Haven project. We furthermore wish to express our appreciation to Joyce Watson, former research analyst in this project, for assistance in data processing. Sincere thanks are due to Dr. Margaret Wheeler, Jane Krisberg, and Marie Donchian of the Neighborhood Improvement Project for a careful reading of the study and helpful criticisms. A special vote of thanks goes to Stella Hanau whose painstaking editorial work and insightful suggestions greatly improved the readability of the manuscript. We also appreciate deeply the responsible secretarial work of Leah Verri and Jemma Plummer.

We wish to thank the editors of *Social Work* and *Marriage and Family Living,* who graciously permitted us to adapt sections of earlier articles for purposes of this book; and the Greater St. Paul Community Chest and Councils, Inc., for allowing us to reproduce a revised version of the Levels of Functioning Scheme, which had first been featured in a Family Centered Project publication. Finally we should like to extend our most sincere appreciation for financial support to the New Haven Foundation and the National Institute of Mental Health, whose grant MH 510-04 made the present study possible.

L. L. G.
M. A. L.

CONTENTS

List of Tables

List of Figures

FOREWORD

Suffering families dealing with the vicissitudes and stresses of an inhospitable world have been the focus of literary themes for centuries, but it has been only recently that the phenomenon of families in trouble has been subjected to systematic research. Today studies of families with problems, problem families, or multi-problem families are being undertaken in many countries and by several different disciplines.

The book by Professor Geismar and Mr. La Sorte which I am introducing in this foreword is the stronger because of the many studies which have preceded it. The authors have not resorted to speculation, to name calling, or to exhortations about problem families which typified many pre-research publications. They have, moreover, gone beyond description of the parameters which characterized early research writings about families in trouble. This treatise draws upon sociological theory to conceptualize the structure and functions of families in an urban society and utilizes this framework to study multi-problem families empirically.

To put the research by Geismar and La Sorte in perspective, we should note that four streams of research on families under stress have been running parallel for some time: (1) studies on families in crisis, including the correlates of crisis-proneness, largely by sociologists; (2) research on families in natural disasters by a variety of social scientists; (3) studies of the interplay of the effects of mental disorders on families and of family disorganization on psychiatric patients by psychiatric researchers; and (4) studies of the properties of the "multi-problem family," mainly by social workers.

The present research, undertaken by sociologists within a social work setting, brings to the fourth category of studies an added theoretical and methodological sophistication which should win acclaim in several disciplines. In my judgment the authors have drawn from the sociologists theory and method, and from the previous work in psychiatry and social work a sensitivity to the problems of diagnosing (including early identification) and treating problem families.

In focusing on the multi-problem family, the authors are contributing to a rapidly growing literature. Covering American, French, Dutch, British, and Commonwealth sources, Benjamin Schlesinger and his associates annotated and reviewed a total of 307 publications since World War II.[1] Perhaps even more startling was the survey by Lagey and Ayres which located 143 community programs in Canada and the United States, organized on behalf of multi-problem families.[2] These should be sufficient indicators of the saliency of the problem among researchers and the social concern that has been built up about treatment.

There is some evidence that the diagnosis and treatment of multi-problem families is becoming a field of specialization in social welfare requiring special skills and competences. This research is, therefore, especially timely.

The authors have set for themselves a number of tasks: (1) definition and identification of the multi-problem family, (2) description and measurement of the degree of malfunctioning in problem families, (3) identification of conditions,

---

[1] Benjamin Schlesinger, *The Multi-Problem Family: A Review and Annotated Bibliography* (Toronto: University of Toronto Press, 1963).

[2] Joseph C. Lagey and Beverly Ayres, *Community Treatment Programs for Multi-Problem Families* (Vancouver, B.C.: Community Chest and Councils of the Greater Vancouver Area, 1962).

settings, and characteristics associated with gross malfunctioning; and (4) implication of findings for diagnosis, treatment, and community services. As can be seen, this constitutes a tour de force in blending theory, methodology and field applications which is rarely achieved in sociological research. It is my conclusion that the authors have carried off their assignment superbly.

At the risk of scooping the authors, let me close this foreword by noting a few findings which merit underlining. They will be adorned and fully documented in the chapters which follow.

First, the authors enable us by their conceptual framework to analyze families as entities in their own right. Instead of focusing on adequacy of individual performances with its accent on the personalities of family members, the family is seen as a functioning association which performs functions for its members and for the community. Taking the eye off the functionaries and focusing on family functions permits analysis of the problematics in the family situation independent of the personalities of its members. Functions can be shown to be shared among several positions within the family, and adequacy of role functioning evaluated by total family performance. In this same vein sharing of functions can be shown to occur between the family and extrafamily agencies. The authors contend that families have not so much specialized as they have shared functions with other agencies. On none of the traditional functions can it be shown that families have been released from their responsibilities by the community.

Second, in assessing malfunctioning among families the authors find evidence that multi-problem families exaggerate the same trends found in single problem families (such as ADC families and many of the short-term families served by family service agencies): namely, that the role functioning at the interior of the family (primarily expressive) is least often adequate; and that the performance on the visible reputation, giving functions of providing and housekeeping (primarily instrumental) which are monitored more effectively by the community, is most frequently adequate.

Third, the authors with the aid of retrospective data, compare stable and disorganized lower-class families on behavior early in the family life cycle. A major finding with implications for early identification of the multi-problem family is the discovery that differences between stable and disorganized families occur early in the family history. A program of aggressive case finding by workers could identify from this discovery incipient problem families early enough to forestall breakdown and disorganization.

Finally, in the syndrome associated with malfunctioning in multiple areas, the authors show that poverty is not a sufficient explanation, that character disorders are not sufficient, and that inadequate neighborhoods are not sufficient to explain this phenomenon. If all these are combined with an impoverished cultural heritage with respect to problem solving, poor intrafamily communication, and a general lack of confidence and trust among members, then the full range of multi-problem families studied appears accounted for.

In the years that have elapsed since the multi-problem family became an object of special study and attention, ways of intervening have been explored and several strategies advanced for coping with families in trouble. The authors evaluate these strategies in the light of their findings and recommend a combination of aggressive case finding and intensive casework coupled with extensive community development. The documentation of their stance involves an artful joining of research findings and action alternatives on behalf of troubled families which in itself commends the book to a wide audience.

REUBEN HILL

CHAPTER  1:

DELINEATING THE PROBLEM

It is no accident that research and social action focused on the disorganized or multi-problem family for the first time during the 1950's. Though earlier decades of the twentieth century witnessed the rapid growth of the social sciences and the development of social work into a full-fledged profession, certain major events during this period overshadowed the crisis situations which occurred in the lives of a small segment of the population. The economic depression of the 1930's and the global war of the forties left little room for society to concern itself with those of its members whose problems, however severe and persistent, were neither felt nor shared by the community at large.

In the postwar period, however, general economic prosperity, broken only by relatively brief recessions, and a rise in the standard of living brought into sharp relief the fate of

15

one portion of our population which did not benefit from the blessings of a booming economy or from the provisions of an improved system of social security. Moreover, the growth process of the social work profession itself, as we shall show, has been a determinant in the shift of focus to, and then away from, problems such as those presented by the multi-problem family.

The supposition held by health and welfare agencies that a small number of families in a given community were beset by a multiplicity of serious problems was supported by several surveys which are cited in subsequent pages. However, what magnified the problem in the eyes of the larger community was the finding from a St. Paul, Minnesota, study done in 1948 that over half of the combined services and budget allotments of the major health and welfare agencies of the city were being absorbed by a small proportion of families which were being served simultaneously by several community welfare resources.[1] Subsequent surveys in St. Paul and a number of other urban communities produced supporting evidence that between two and three per cent of the families in the community are seriously disorganized, take up the bulk of social services, and also account for a disproportionate share of deviant behavior, such as abuse and neglect of children, juvenile delinquency, adult crime, and adult alcoholism.

An analysis of the use of social services made by these families reveals that their relationships with agencies have been poor, ranging from indifferent to hostile. Most of these families are known by their pattern of going from agency to agency, in search of one which will meet their immediate need. Agencies note that the families make repeated application for service but fail to follow through with the plans offered to help them. The relationships of the multi-problem families to the community can best be described as "anomic," that is, as having a lack of identification with and integration into the community, and a nonadherence to community values. The relationships which they do have lack the strength and stability necessary for healthy identification. Contacts with the neighborhood are tenuous. There is little participation in church, school, and recreational activities. A mutual alienation appears to be characteristic of the relationship between the community agencies or institutions and these families.

Public welfare agencies and those providing correctional and protective services have been most aware of the existence of the multi-problem family. Although rarely analyzed in conceptual terms, such a family is characterized by recidivism, deviant behavior, frequency of crisis situations, and chronicity of assistance and services. The last named has taken strikingly tangible form in voluminous case records going back frequently over several generations.

The ever-growing concern of the American social work community with the multi-problem family has led the authors of this volume to attempt a systematic analysis of its functioning and an exploration of ways in which social welfare might move toward prevention of the problems the family presents to the community and to itself. An effort has been made to present the disorganized family within a framework of classifications which is consistent with leading concepts on the nature of the American family system, drawn from both social science and social work. The particular conceptual approach used here was selected for its pertinence to treatment planning at various levels of community organization.

The contents in this book are drawn from a number of studies, particularly the research done in the Neighborhood Improvement Project of New Haven, Connecticut, and the Family Centered Project of St. Paul, Minn. Chapters 4 and 5 comprise a detailed report on a New Haven study comparing a group of disorganized families in a public housing project with a group of stable families in the same project. Comparisons encompass contrasts in present patterns of social functioning and in modes of behavior early in the family life cycle. The main theme of this study is the development of knowledge which may lead to an early identification of the multi-problem family.

The authors' general purpose is to give the reader a conceptual clarification of the multi-problem family and an acquaintance with data on the subject that have been uncovered by research, and thus enable him to gain a better understanding of a problem whose urgency has come to be acknowledged by the social work profession and many communities throughout the country.

A QUESTION OF TERMINOLOGY

The term "multi-problem family" appears to the authors to be the most appropriate term by which to designate the phenomenon discussed in this volume. In view of the fact that many papers and articles on the subject of problem families dispose of the question of terminology as being of minor importance (after all, what's in a name?) we deemed it necessary to discuss the concept in its larger perspective, that is, to consider the term "multi-problem family" from the viewpoint of its conceptual adequacy.

A heightened awareness of, and concern with, the problems of the seriously disorganized family have led public and private welfare agencies all over the nation to establish projects and services on behalf of these families. A survey by the State Charities Aid Association listed ten different programs in the state of New York alone.[2] No complete roster of such undertakings for the entire country seems to be available at this writing (1962), but a survey by the Community Chest and Councils of the Greater Vancouver (B.C.) area revealed that as of 1962, at least 143 communities out of 260 surveyed in the United States and Canada are engaged in some kind of activity designed to cope with the problem of the multi-problem family.[3] There is practically no communication among these undertakings, and most of them appear to be struggling on their own without the benefit of knowledge and findings from other communities. The growing concern with the problems of such families is also expressed by the increasing number of sessions devoted to the subject at national and regional welfare conferences.

It would appear from all these activities that this area of concern is in the process of becoming a major field of practice in social welfare. In the face of this situation, the question arises whether the lack of adequate terminology and definitions does not represent a major obstacle to the development of such a field of social work practice.

A number of descriptive terms have been used in the literature to designate the seriously disorganized family. They include hard-core, socially delinquent, deprived, distrustful, hard-to-reach, and others. Each in its way singles out for description a given characteristic of these families. The term "multi-problem family" has perhaps been used more widely than the other designations. Yet, referring as it does to problems rather than to specific family traits, the term poses some problems of its own with regard to definition.

Without disclaiming the possibility of independent invention, the authors recall that the expression "multi-problem family" was first proposed as a descriptive term for seriously disorganized families by Isaac Hoffman, Research Director of the Wilder Foundation in St. Paul, Minnesota, in connection with the 1948 St. Paul study, noted above. The term was adopted by the survey team for this study, entitled the *Family Unit Report Study,* carried out under the auspices of Community Research Associates, Inc., of New

York. In this survey the term was used to designate families with serious problems in more than one of the following areas: social adjustment, health, economic behavior, and recreational need.[4]

The obvious difficulty with this definition is its vagueness. As seen in the *Family Unit Report Study* a problem was a pathological condition which needed treatment. The border-line between pathology and normal behavior is difficult to delineate. Furthermore, the four areas designated are so broad that a breakdown in only one of the areas might result in a serious impairment of the family's capacity to function as a unit. Yet in the view of many practitioners, the term "multi-problem" seems suggestive enough of certain characteristics and behavior patterns found in family disorganization to merit continued use when defined more sharply.

The Family Centered Project of St. Paul, which was one of the intended outgrowths of the *Family Unit Report Study,* concentrated much of its research work upon an effort to develop a conceptual foundation for studying the nature of, and the giving of service to, the multi-problem family. This effort was perceived as a precondition for any attempt to evaluate the work with multi-problem families. The definition of multi-problem family, developed in the Family Centered Project and refined in the New Haven Neighborhood Improvement Project, and the general conceptual framework in which the definition is cast serve as a base for the present discussion of the work with, and findings about, multi-problem families.

The term "multi-problem family," as used in this book, denotes a family with disorganized social functioning of an order that adversely affects the following sets of behavior: (1) relationships inside the family; (2) relationships outside the family group, particularly neighborhood and community relationships; and (3) the performance of tasks such as those concerned with health, and with economic and household practices that are designed to maintain the family as a physical unit. To our mind, the value of defining the multi-problem family in this way lies in the relatedness of the definition to social practice and its potential for measurement.

The adequacy of a concept can be judged only in relation to its uses. In this instance we needed to ask ourselves what are the specific purposes which might be served by the concept and definition selected. The purposes may be summarized under the following headings: (1) understanding of family functioning, (2) identification, (3) diagnosis, (4) treatment, and (5) evaluation of change. The present volume is chiefly concerned with the first two purposes and with the search for a method leading to early detection of multi-problem behavior.

NOTES FOR CHAPTER 1

[1] Bradley Buell and Associates, *Community Planning for Human Services* (New York: Columbia University Press, 1952), pp. 9 ff.

[2] State Charities Aid Association, *"Multi-Problem Families," a New Name or a New Problem?* (New York: State Charities Aid Association, May, 1960).

[3] Joseph C. Lagey and Beverly Ayres, *Community Treatment Programs for Multi-Problem Families* (Vancouver Community Chest and Councils of the Greater Vancouver Area, Dec. 1962), pp. 1-6.
See also Joseph C. Lagey and Beverly Ayres, "Community Treatment Programs for Multi-Problem Families," in Benjamin Schlesinger, *The Multi-Problem Family, A Review and Annotated Bibliography* (Toronto: University of Toronto Press, 1963), pp. 55-71.

[4] Bradley Buell and Associates, *op. cit.*, pp. 9-11.

CHAPTER  2:

TOWARD CONCEPTUAL
CLARIFICATION

FAMILY DISORGANIZATION
IN PERSPECTIVE

Little would be gained in our present effort if we treated the problem of family disorganization as if it constituted a newly discovered phenomenon in the history of social science and social action. This is far from being the case. Ernest Mowrer wrote in 1927: "Almost within the last generation the family has come into public consciousness as the matrix of a growing social problem."[1] Thomas and Znaniecki studied the disintegration of the Polish family in America.[2] Cavan and Ranck[3] and Angell[4] did research on family disorganization resulting from economic depression.

Since the 1930's it has become commonplace for writers of textbooks on social disorganization to treat the problems of the family as an integral part of the larger social process. What is new, however, is the professional concern of social work with the problem.

There appears to be a general consensus among these investigators, but one not necessarily perceived or accepted by society as a whole, that events like separation, desertion, divorce, widowhood, delinquency, and crime do not constitute social disorganization *per se* but are merely symptoms of this process. As such they may serve as rough indices of family disorganization and are subject to careful examination as to their significance relative to the total problem posed. The loose use of divorce statistics, for instance, has given rise to much unfounded speculation about the future of the American family. Despite the postwar upward trend of divorces, serious students have found little evidence that the family in the United States is moving toward dissolution.

Mowrer and Koos have concerned themselves with the problem of the stability of the modern family. Mowrer stressed the loss of family consciousness and shared interest found in family disorganization;[5] Koos, in addition to the above, regarded the absence of complementary roles and of family goals as important criteria in the disorganization process.[6] The functional analysis approach to the family spelled out in the writings of Parsons and Bales,[7] Bell and Vogel,[8] and others permits an analysis of family stability versus disorganization in terms of the roles of family members in their internal activities and their relationships to other social systems. This approach, because it relates behavior to the social structure, is seen as most promising in our effort to seek ways in which society in general and the social welfare community in particular may cope with the problem of family disorganization.

The question of etiology or cause of family disorganization has been handled less successfully than the description of the phenomenon.

Various societies throughout the ages have advanced explanations of why individuals or families suffer from poverty, ill health, lack of education, and maladjustment.[9] Early civilizations saw supernatural forces at work. Following the Protestant Reformation, a formulation of the theory of poverty and related phenomena in terms of "predestination" gained ground. God's grace upon man was seen as demonstrated on this earth as well as in the afterlife. Those who received the grace were blessed with wealth and affluence on earth. The poor by contrast were devoid of the grace of God.

In the wake of the growing industrialization of Europe and the concomitant impoverishment of the population working in factory cities, two "scientific" explanations of human poverty and misery gained ground. The first of these, Neo-Darwinism, a restatement of Malthus' earlier argument on overpopulation, postulated that the survival of the fittest applied not only to the animal world but to man as well. Poverty, disease, and even war were seen as nature's way of improving the race. The weak and the unfit were eliminated by higher morbidity and mortality which, however cruel in their manifestations, were seen to benefit mankind in the long run.

A contrary theory was put forth by Marx and Engels in their *Communist Manifesto* (1848) and the impact of their thinking continues to be felt to this day. Poverty and misery, they argued, are the result of exploitation of the working class by the owners of the means of production. The remedy for this evil is the equitable distribution of society's property and wealth. Such equality could be achieved by a revolutionary process in which the working class takes over the means of production.

Since Marx and Engels first stated their proposition the

standard of living in many industrialized nations has risen more than fourfold, and with this rise has come a drastic improvement of the lot of the working class. This fact and the advance in welfare legislation in nearly all industrialized nations have weakened the argument that poverty and other forms of deprivation are simply the result of exploitation. In an economy of nearly full employment and a considerable range of social services it has come somewhat as a shock to learn that a large minority of the population has not benefited from the improvement in living conditions which has come to the population as a whole.

In more recent years students of the phenomena of human poverty and misery have reached the conclusion that protracted economic dependency and problem functioning, extending often over several generations, cannot be the product of poverty alone. There has emerged instead the concept of personal and social disorganization which is broader and more complex than poverty. The concept implies a breakdown in the process of social organization and postulates multiple causes for the families' failure to adjust to society.

Various disciplines, though tacitly acknowledging multiple causation, have tended to stress factors inherent in their own pursuits as being predominant in the causation of problem behavior. Intelligence testing by the U.S. Army in World War I and findings of IQ differences among ethnic groups gave rise to explanations of differences in intellectual endowment which have their origin in biological factors. These findings were then applied on a broad scale as causal elements in crime, delinquency, poverty, and social inadequacy. The genealogical case studies of the Juke and Kallikak families, for instance, supported the thesis that social inadequacy was a product of biological forces, including limited intelligence.

Freudian theory of personality genesis made a heavy

impact upon the prevailing thinking about causes of human behavior beginning in the 1920's. In stressing the importance of early developmental stages in the formation of personality, Freudian concepts did much to shift the burden of "responsibility" from purely biological factors to psychological processes. The Freudian formulation made it necessary to spell out the role of society in the genesis of deviant behavior. Yet, there was a tendency, especially in America, where deeply rooted concepts of moral inadequacy as the source of poverty and inadequacy were widespread, to interpret the Freudian formulation as a theory of personal (psychological) inadequacy without sufficient regard for the social realities the individual had to face.[10]

In the 1930's, sociologists under the leadership of Park and Burgess carried out studies which showed that social disorganization tends to be confined to certain slum areas in the city. Moreover, they found that whereas given ethnic groups who left the slums were able to improve their social situation, high rates of delinquency, crime, and economic deprivation tended to remain a characteristic of the area no matter which ethnic group inhabited it. More recently sociologists and social psychologists engaged in the study of delinquency [11] and mental disorder [12] have sought to demonstrate an interrelationship between behavior pathology and social structure.

The more recent trend in explaining disorganized behavior is to use a multi-causal framework as a basis for theory and research. This is particularly well illustrated in Alexander Leighton's community studies in Nova Scotia done under the auspices of Cornell University.[13] The bio-psycho-social approach to an understanding of behavior and disorganization has been gaining ground in the helping professions (psychiatry, social work, public health) as well as in the social sciences proper. However, it would appear that the psychogenic approach which explains behavior problems chiefly in terms of a person's experiences in infancy and early childhood continue to be widely held among professional practitioners.

During the late 1950's and early 1960's students of the problem of poverty, particularly economists and anthropologists, have pointed to the consistently high correlation between economic deprivation and various types of deviant behavior such as crime and delinquency, mental illness, physical illness and handicaps, alcoholism, drug addiction, and many other forms of social maladjustment. The concept "culture of poverty," which has gained increasing currency, has come to refer to a self-perpetuating way of life which circumscribes much of human behavior and sets serious limits to a person's opportunity for eluding its grip. Adherents of the culture-of-poverty theory have maintained that an attack upon misery and deviant behavior will be effective only to the extent that social action can succeed in modifying the culture and the system of values which sustains it.

Society's ways of dealing with human poverty and misery have naturally been influenced by current social philosophies and theories about etiology. Thus it is pertinent to consider briefly the development of social work from its early preprofessional days to the present time.

The pre-professional era of social work was characterized by an undifferentiated approach to human deprivation. The name of the "Society for the Prevention of Pauperism and Crime" which functioned in London in 1864 provides an illustration of the way society viewed the underprivileged.[14] The English Poor Law, whose origin dates back to the sixteenth century, had already established a tradition of dealing with those members of society who were unable to care for themselves. Typical ways of handling the problem of poverty and indigency included giving charity relief, visitation to the poor by respectable citizens, and simply isolating the victims in hospitals, almshouses, jails, and workhouses. Even prior to the Reformation religious bodies had developed measures of extending charity to the "unfortunate poor" on a local (manor, parish, or other religious community) basis.

A most significant step toward differentiated treatment occurred in England during the second half of the nineteenth century "around the development of specialized care for various groups of needy people, sick, children, aged and infirm, insane, feeble-minded, blind, etc." [15] Concurrently with a growing specialization in service there was a shift in responsibility for meeting welfare needs, from religious and local authorities to the state. This trend reached its full expression in the German Social Security Act of 1883 which provided compulsory insurance for sickness and maternity, and later added provisions for protection against income loss due to invalidism, disabling injury, and old age.[16] The Social Security Act in the United States, passed in 1935, had been preceded by similar measures in a number of other Western nations.

Early social work practice in the United States was characterized mainly by social services to the dependent, although the philosophy, values, and mores of American life prior to the Civil War left its imprint upon the development of modern social work. Cohen states:

> Concern for such concepts as individualism, democracy, and humanitarianism was becoming deeply inbedded in the mores of the nation, and the resultant attitudes toward the needs, rights, and responsibilities of the individual and of government have affected the course and direction of social welfare programs, both private and public, to this day.[17]

Around the turn of this century social work in the United States began to steer a new course, away from the concern with the moral behavior of the underprivileged and toward a program of environmental improvement as the means for reaching a solution to the problems of poverty, dependency, and disease. Education, legislation, and surveys were the more common means for effecting change which would lead to a betterment of conditions under which people lived.[18]

During the first half of the century, the field of social welfare moved increasingly from an undifferentiated stage toward social welfare programs in highly specialized or fragmented forms.[19] It is noteworthy, however, that pioneers of the profession such as Mary Richmond and Jane Addams were advocates of an integrated approach in diagnosis and treatment and put stress on the interrelationship between the problems of the individual and the pathology of the groups in which he lived such as family, neighborhood, community, and society.

Following World War I the influence of Freudian psychology was keenly felt in the profession.

> Social work turned to psychiatry for help in developing a method of dealing with the individual who was facing problems of maladjustment. It took over, however, more than a method of treatment! It took over also a view of the nature of man and his social arrangements. It saw personal anxieties and maladjustment as rooted in the individual and his psychological past to the neglect of "structural" maladjustment—that is, maladjustment rooted in "quite objective social disorders." Concern for social institutions was almost neglected in the naïve belief that if one worked with enough individuals the social institutions would indirectly improve.[20]

The depression of the thirties once again shifted the focus of social welfare to the "external" realities of American life, particularly to the problems of safeguarding a large portion of the population from the ravages of unemployment, disability, old age, and other potential crisis situations. Government had begun to move into social welfare on a large scale, and there was again increasing concern with the role of society in treating individuals.

The professionalization of social work gave rise to the new subdisciplines of group work and community organization which, in contrast to casework, drew heavily upon sociological and social-psychological theory for the formulation of treatment programs. The trend during the past decade has been toward broader and less specialized agency programs and toward a more integrated, community-wide approach toward welfare services. This trend has in part been strengthened by the recognition of the phenomenon of the multi-problem family. Such families had been encountered earlier but had not been separately identified. The greater emphasis upon social factors in the search for causation has sparked epidemiological studies on family disorganization such as those undertaken by Community Research Associates, Inc., the New York Youth Board, the St. Paul Family Centered Project, and other organizations.

A common finding in these studies is the concentration of various types of problem functioning such as economic dependency, delinquency, social maladjustment, and mental illness in a relatively small group of families and frequently in a few areas of a community. A general limitation in the studies done up to the present time is their reliance on behavior already known to the community rather than on all types of problem functioning. It is recognized that studies relying on officially reported behavior are less efficient in delineating the total scope of the problem than they are in showing points of concentration in the incidence of problematic functioning.

To sum up the foregoing discussion: Pre-professional social work tended to lump together, for purposes of diagnosis and treatment, problem behavior of the most diverse kinds. Diagnosis, of course, constituted no more than a classification by behavior symptoms, whereas treatment was largely determined by the degree to which welfare bodies wished to extend charity or impose punishment and isolation upon those who failed to live up to the standards of society. The beginnings of professional social work were noted for their strong accent on social aspects in the diagnosis and the services provided to clients. As a result, social workers, in serving families and neighborhoods, had considerable awareness of the interplay of problem functioning, particularly in deprived neighborhoods. Much of this focus, however, was lost in the process of agency specialization and service fragmentation, and under the influence of a theoretical orientation which put major stress upon psychological individualization.

The return swing of the treatment and service pendulum in social work toward broader and more integrated service programs and a more eclectic interpretation of human behavior permitted the more ready identification of multiproblem behavior and the establishment of co-ordinated family centered and neighborhood centered programs of treatment.

Many of these programs have been handicapped by the lack of a conceptual approach to the problem. Conceptualization may be seen as a first step in delineating the nature and scope of the problem, planning treatment, and evaluating its consequences. In the long run a good conceptual approach holds promise of dealing with the question of causation which is the most fruitful avenue toward an eventual program aimed at prevention.

FAMILY PROBLEMS AND PROBLEM FAMILIES

Most public and many private agencies have known multiproblem families in their case loads and given some service to them for years. What is new is the quickly growing and widely publicized concern over these families' failure to respond to conventional treatment methods and a concerted effort by some communities to meet the problem head-on.

Social surveys have provided ample evidence that the multi-problem family takes more than its proportionate share of welfare funds, services, and supplies, and contributes more than its share of juvenile delinquents, neglect cases, alcoholism, and other types of adult deviant behavior.[21]

There is general agreement that the multi-problem family is the "family in trouble," but there is less agreement on the exact universe of families falling into the multi-problem group. Different programs devoted to service and research set up different definitions of what constitutes a multi-problem family.

The St. Paul Family Unit Report Study, as noted above, defined the multi-problem family as one with serious problems in more than one of the four basic areas of family life: social adjustment, health, economic behavior, and recreational need. The Family Centered Project in St. Paul applied the same criterion for the initial selection of cases to be treated but added the additional condition of children in "clear and present danger," defined as a situation where the immediate welfare of the children is being threatened to the extent that the community has a clear-cut responsibility to intervene.[22]

The authors of a report by the State Charities Aid Association of New York, who surveyed a number of papers and articles from community projects in the state, were able to tease out the following criteria for multi-problem families: (1) multiplicity of problems, (2) chronicity of need, (3) resistance to treatment, and (4) handicapping attitudes.[23] The last criterion refers to attitudes which hinder integration in the community at large, such as hostility to, indifference toward, or lack of respect for, authorities, services, and agency programs.

Two themes appear to run through practically all the

descriptions of the families and definitions of the concept in papers, articles, and books dealing with the subject. The first states that the multi-problem family is plagued by many serious problems which it cannot handle by itself or through the services made available by the community; the second indicates that the family has repeatedly come to the attention of the community and that the nature of the contact with communal organizations, agencies, and authorities has been predominantly negative. This negative quality is generally described by such adjectives as nonco-operative, resistant, and hostile.

A problem can be viewed as a situation which is harmful to the organism and/or group and which needs readjustment. All families have problems. Indeed mature living represents a continuous process of problem solving and adjustment to changing relationships and situations.

Some families have more serious problems than others, but such problems need not lead to family disorganization. Sibling rivalry is a common phenomenon which may be handled with a certain amount of understanding and social skill. A protracted illness of a parent may put a great strain upon family stability. There may be disagreements between husband and wife, financial debts, acting out of children, and illness of a family member, simultaneously or in succession. Any family experiencing some or all of these situations may be said to have real family problems, but it does not thereby necessarily turn into a multi-problem family, as the term is understood here.

To illustrate: Family A, a hypothetical example, is a working-class family with five children, two of whom show symptoms of malnutrition. The oldest boy, a young teenager, has recently been accepted for diagnostic services by the mental hygiene clinic because of repeated truancy. The parents had not known of the nutritional problems of the children, but once made aware of them they have cooperated closely with the Visiting Nurses to remedy the situation. The boy's truancy had concerned them greatly, and they themselves had sought the advice of the principal regarding appropriate services. Presently, both mother and child are undergoing treatment at the community sponsored clinic. The father also has participated in a number of treatment sessions. Family A is clearly not a multi-problem family. It has serious family problems, to be sure, but the parents have taken the initiative and have shown strength in coping with the situation. Whether or not they have the means to pay for the services needed is not a consideration in this context.

The first theme in defining the multi-problem family, as noted above, implies that the problems the family has encountered are threatening its well-being and perhaps the welfare of society, and that these problems have not lent themselves to a solution through the action taken or supported by members of the family itself. The second theme denotes a situation which is problematic to the community as well as to the family. Having come to the attention of the community does not mean that the family has come to request the much-needed service. For our purposes, coming to the attention of the community is taken to mean that the family has become a special and well-known case to agencies. The family is identified because of the trouble it has given to agencies. This has taken manifold forms, such as repeated requests for service without follow-through in the face of great need, an aggressively demanding attitude but little readiness to review the family situation with the agency, or extreme apathy toward any services or course of action suggested by the agency to solve or ameliorate serious family problems. Thus we find that in addition to the existence of multiple problems, the family's perception and handling of these problems are crucial to the concept of the multi-problem family. It is this latter consideration that differentiates the family with problems from the problem family.

Unquestionably, there is interaction between the nature of the problems and the family's relationship to them. Serious problems of any kind in a family situation test the ability of family members to tolerate social and emotional stress and to mobilize their own resources to cope with the problems. The more serious the problems are, the greater the ego strength or interpersonal competence required in order to prevent breakdown in the personality structure or in the social organization of the family.

Multi-problem families evidence apathy toward over-all family problems and hostility toward the agent offering help. Factors other than family crisis are, of course, at the root of such behavior, but they are likely to take latent rather than manifest forms in the absence of real stress.

Chronicity of need, which was cited as one of the four criteria for defining the multi-problem family in the report of the State Charities Aid Association,[24] is very frequently associated with family disorganization. It is questionable whether chronicity of need itself may be considered a necessary condition for defining a family situation as multi-problem. There may, of course, be a correlation between chronicity of need and magnitude, as well as pervasiveness, of problems. However, the authors know many multi-problem families in which the multiplicity of problems and the families' failure to face them and work toward a solution came into existence in a relatively short period of time. In other words, a family may develop all the characteristics of multi-problem behavior in a span of time as short as one year.

The time factor in diagnosing families as multi-problem is, of course, far from irrelevant. Chronic problems often erupt into a crisis, which may be defined as a situation of severe social and/or emotional stress. However, it is the consequences of the crisis rather than the crisis itself which determine whether a family will remain stable or become disorganized. In the event that a family experiences great shock or tragedy, a measure of disorganization may be the inevitable result. At the point of crisis the time factor is likely to differentiate between two types of families: those which are able to cope with their problems and to recuperate, and those which become so disorganized that they do not provide adequately for the physical, social, and emotional needs of their members. The multi-problem family belongs, of course, in the second category. Its characteristic manner of meeting a crisis is that of permanent or repeated breakdown in the performance of those basic functions which are necessary for the welfare of the family group and its individual members.

TWO RELATED ASPECTS OF MULTI-PROBLEM FUNCTIONING

Far-reaching and promising efforts by social scientists and psychiatrists to build a conceptual basis for studying the family have as yet failed to yield reliable models for an evaluation of family situations in relation to need for social services.[25] The most successful client evaluation studies have confined themselves to an assessment of the behavior or adjustment of individuals receiving treatment.[26] The conceptual approach to the study of the multi-problem family presented here makes no claim to being a theoretical system. The approach utilizes certain known theoretical formulations relative to the roles of the family and its members for purposes of setting up a model. A model is seen, in the words of Loeb, as "the organization of the theory-derived processes and categories which appear to be related to the problem." [27]

This model utilizes the concept family functioning or social functioning of the family. In the field of social work the term social functioning, as employed by Werner

Boehm,[28] has tended to become a unifying concept which makes it possible to relate human behavior to professional intervention. Functioning can be defined in Blaine Mercer's terms simply as "the processes associated with the structure." [29] These processes may serve to protect the structure and contribute to its order change or they may lead to its weakening and even destruction (malfunctioning). The term functioning is used here mainly in relation to the family.

It should be noted that the term "disorganized family" is used synonymously with the term "multi-problem family" in the following discussion and throughout this book. The family is conceptualized as a system or aggregate of interdependent parts with an underlying degree of organization. The parts of the family system are social roles that are reciprocally related and interactive, relative to more or less clearly or vaguely defined goals. Family disorganization denotes failure in the organization of the system. Such failure indicates in a general way that the roles of the system are not integrated and do not work together to ensure the maintenance of the system. There are a number of reasons why roles may not be integrated and why, as a result, the family may be disorganized. These reasons are dealt with on a conceptual basis in this section and in greater detail in the following chapter.

The problem here is one of adequate characterization of the multi-problem family for purposes of diagnosis, treatment, and evaluation of change. The choice of the family as the unit of diagnosis and treatment presupposes the use of an evaluative model which is likewise centered upon the family. The family in the United States represents a group of two or more people who are related by blood, marriage, or adoption and who reside together.[30] The American family presents a number of definable attributes. It is an aggregate of interacting individuals who view themselves as being part of the group called a family; and its members perform social roles which may be seen as implementing the functions assigned to the family.

These functions provide the clue to an understanding of the nature of the family and to any effort to diagnose and treat families which have encountered problems. The functions of the American family are difficult to define because of the variations in expectations existing from one subculture to another, and also because of the changes in expectations occurring in time. Functions on which the American family has a monopoly have been decreasing over the past generations, and more functions have come to be shared with other groups in society. It appears that of the former category only four remain allocated specifically to the modern family: reproduction, shelter and physical care for family members, emotional care, and the socialization of the young. Other functions such as economic practices, treatment of illness, education, and recreation have come to be shared to an increasing degree with other organizations in society.

Despite the reduced number of monopoly functions assigned to the family by the American culture, there are a variety of tasks which the family is expected to carry out in order to give its members a sense of belonging to, and identification with, the family. These tasks are deemed especially important in the socialization of children. Thus, in spite of the wide prevalence of social and recreational facilities, the family is expected to provide a home where a member can find warmth and affection, a setting for relaxation and play with friends, and other advantages. Although medicine has become highly specialized, the family is expected to take care of its ill members in the home unless the treatment requires facilities and services available only at a hospital. The home is still considered a preferred eating place for the family, even for the financially well-endowed, albeit cities and towns are dotted with good eating places.

The family as a universal social group, anthropologists have long observed, is charged with certain basic tasks which are carried out by means of a division of labor or allocation of tasks. Tasks are allocated by roles (sets of activities or behavior viewed as belonging together) assigned to various members of a family. A person's social adjustment has much to do with whether or not he actually plays the role expected of him.

As we set about describing and understanding the family and its situation, we become aware of two aspects of its functioning on which we may focus in order to gain a meaningful picture.

On the one hand, we may inquire into the roles each family member plays and try to answer such questions as whether the roles are in line with expectations of other family members, neighbors, the social class or community to which the family belongs. We may ask whether the various roles each member plays are consistent or contradictory or in conflict with each other. The answers to these questions will tell us something about how a given family member is adjusted and gets along in life.

On the other hand, we may ask different kinds of questions focusing on functions. We may wish to know whether certain tasks or functions which a family is supposed to carry out are actually being performed, and how well this is being done. In raising such questions we are not unmindful of the fact that the various family functions, which can be defined as activities in relation to given goals, are fulfilled by family members. Yet, the focus on functions rather than functionaries permits analysis of the family situation independent of the personalities of its members.

That there is some relationship between family members' personalities and the manner in which the functions are discharged can hardly be questioned.[31] Yet, in our view of the family as a social system composed of many individual roles, the manner in which functions are performed and the way family members behave cannot be considered synonymous. After all, any family may be burdened by members who have shortcomings of one sort or another which are likely to affect adversely the functioning of the family in given areas. Some families, however, are able to marshal resources for having these functions taken over by family members other than the one conventionally entrusted with the task. Our inquiry at the level of social functioning is concerned with how well the task is performed rather than with who performs it. What emerges here is a dual focus for viewing and describing the family.

In the first instance we see the family as being composed of individuals, each of whom plays a large number of roles. The man, for instance, may play the roles of husband, father, head of the house, manager of the family budget, income provider, worker at the factory, union member, member of the volunteer fire department and bowling league. The woman would tend to play the roles of wife, mother, homemaker, dispenser of home nursing care, member of the PTA, member of a sewing club, or other group. Similar patterns of roles could be enumerated for the children in the home. These role patterns or sets, as has been stated above, must be integrated around the person if he is to function normally. In looking at all the family members and studying their patterns of role performance, some picture about the nature of the family comes to light.

In the second instance we can view the family relative to the way family functions are carried out. These functions represent the convergence of roles or activities performed by family members with the object of accomplishing a certain task. Some functions are monopolized by one member of the family. Others represent a true joining of roles by two or more family members. Budgeting, for example, may take either form. Raising of children is likely to be a shared activity involving the roles of the husband, wife, and perhaps one or more older siblings.

It should be kept in mind that just as the personality represents a joining of individual roles around the person or self, the performance of tasks or functions constitutes a meeting of roles in relation to a goal. In the latter case, however, the roles tend to issue from several family members. They form an aggregate not attached to one person but to several persons brought together in a common task. Like the role pattern around the self, the aggregate of task centered or function centered roles needs to be integrated if the functions are to be performed well. By integration we mean that roles need to be compatible, mutually complementary, and geared to the same goal.

In looking at the array of roles that family members play, we can distinguish two groupings, relative to the nature of the roles: (1) a group that may be differentiated according to whether the roles are performed within or outside the home and (2) a group that may be differentiated according to the functions of the roles. Role playing within the family usually takes place in the home, but individuals from the age of nursery school onward tend to divide their role performance between home and various settings outside the home. The division, which varies from family to family and from one socio-economic class to another, is influenced by the expectations about the role.

A situation in which roles are divided in a way which differs sharply from expectations may give rise to conflicts of various kinds. The man who stays home instead of going to work, regardless of whether he can financially afford to be idle, faces disdain from his family, friends, and neighbors. The husband who works in town but who is seldom home, whether because of his work schedule or because of his private social life, may incur the resentment of his wife and children. The mother who absents herself excessively from the home, whatever the reasons, is considered to neglect her responsibility of wife and mother.

The nature of the role predetermines to a large extent whether it is to be performed within or outside the home. The balance in time and frequency between the two sets of roles depends on a great many factors including sex, age, occupation, and personality traits of family members. Since the two sets of role performance are played by the same people, they are probably not unrelated. The question of relatedness of role sets is a rather important one in family diagnosis. Most of the roles played away from home are much more visible than those played in the home, in the sense that visibility refers to the capacity of outsiders to make observations on a person's functioning.

The teacher at school is in a position to observe and understand the behavior of the child; the foreman at work is able to gain some impression about the adjustment of the head of the family; the recreation worker can gather relevant information about the problems of the teen-ager. By contrast, roles played within the family are largely hidden from view of nonmembers except in instances where professional intervention has provided the opportunity to assess intrafamilial roles.

The utility of drawing a distinction between the two role sets—those within and those outside the family—is contained in the assumed diagnostic value of the more visible role performance in relation to all family functioning. The problem of testing the empirical evidence will be taken up later. A further value in drawing this distinction lies in the possibility of studying families in relation to their degree of integration in larger social system, that is, the neighborhood and community.

In the second grouping of roles of family members a differentiation can be made between what Parsons and Bales call expressive and instrumental functions.[32] This distinction has to do with whether actions are aimed primarily at regulating the internal affairs of the family and maintaining a pattern of relationships which satisfies the emotional needs of its members (expressive), or whether actions are geared chiefly to the problem of relations between the family and situations outside the family system. The latter functions, moreover, are geared to meeting family needs relative to its biophysical existence, such as the health and economic welfare of its members.

The differentiation between roles representing instrumental and expressive functions would seem to be a meaningful one in any analysis aimed at understanding the nature of family members' involvement in family life. The relative amount of participation of members in both sets of roles and changes in the pattern of such participation would seem to give an indication of the quality of family life, family cohesiveness, the values around which the family is integrated or fails to be integrated, the assumption of responsibility for performing family tasks, et cetera.

Up to this point we have proposed as an over-all conceptual framework that a plausible way of viewing and comprehending the multi-problem family is to study the pattern of roles each family member performs and to analyze the way in which family functions are performed by one or more members of a family. Unanswered as yet is the question of what specific functions we are concerned with when setting about to study the seriously disorganized or multi-problem family. Any scheme selected for research ought to be adapted to the particular universe of behavior exhibited by the families to be studied.

EVALUATION AS A SOCIAL
WORK RESPONSIBILITY

Social work shares with the other helping professions concerned with psychosocial functioning a feeling of inadequacy regarding its ability to evaluate the effects of services rendered. Admittedly, there are good reasons for this situation. Unlike medicine, social work does not deal with conditions which have been diagnosed by precise scientific procedures. This lack of precision makes assessment of change more difficult. The development of skills to cope with problems in behavior has lagged because of the underdevelopment of the behavioral sciences as a whole. In the absence of reliable methods of classification and diagnosis, modes of procedure aimed at inducing changes could not be tested for their efficacy in producing these ends.

It is not within the scope of this section to consider the rather complex conditions accounting for the relatively underdeveloped state of the behavioral sciences. We are more concerned with the fact that the social work profession tends to view its present state of "disability" with a degree of resignation. This attitude is expressed in frequent statements pointing to the lack of clarity in concepts as barriers to systematic studies, and citing the overwhelming obstacles to evaluation research. The arguments given are generally valid, but the attitude of resignation is a bar to the development of the profession. The road to greater theoretical and conceptual clarity lies in part, at least, in research aimed at accurate description of social situation and process. A commitment to this goal and continuance of cumulative efforts in this direction tend to give rise to increasing sophistication in measurement and evaluation and to provide an essential feedback for the growth of social theory.

Application of these premises to the problems raised in the present volume reveals that a situation which is sometimes described as a "service orientation" prevails to the exclusion of a research approach. A helping profession can obviously not function without a service orientation. It constitutes the most essential ingredient of the process and value system of the social work profession. Yet the commitment to a service orientation that remains unmatched by a research orientation leaves little hope for the establishment of the much-needed scientific base for social work.

We realize that evaluation of the results of services given lies at the heart of any attempt to test the utility of the services and to move toward an improvement of those services already in existence. Evaluation in this context covers three facets: (1) clearly defining the services that are being rendered; (2) showing the changes brought about in the clients who received these services or, more specifically, indicating the positions at which the client stood before and after treatment; and (3) establishing whether the changes were actually the result of the services given.

The first requires a careful assessment of services and their differentiation from other services considered for control purposes. The third is largely a question of adequate research design. The second, with which we shall concern ourselves here, depends upon one's ability to translate a theoretical scheme into operational terms which make evaluation feasible.

Given the conceptual framework of family functioning outlined earlier, it may be asked whether such a scheme provides us with a basis for making any judgment relative to the "goodness" or adequacy of behavior. The mere mention of such an attempt is likely to rouse the ire of many a graduate social worker with a newly acquired awareness that it took the profession several decades to cut itself loose from the judgmental approach which characterized its early beginnings. Does what we are proposing here, he might ask, not lead us back to the social work middle ages when the well-intentioned worker sought to remake the client in the image of a culture not plagued by ignorance, poverty, and maladjustment?

The growth of psychodynamic theory has radically modified the nature of social work since those early days. We have learned a great deal about the structure of personality, motivation, the nature of learning, and other subjects relevant to an understanding of the conditions under which the behavior is being modified. At the same time, anthropology and sociology have strengthened the profession's awareness of behavior differences related to different standards and value systems and have demonstrated the close relationship between culture and human personality.

The evolution of social work under the influence of psychological and social sciences led to the acceptance of a credo which acknowledged the unique qualities of each individual and his right to self-determination. Such an articulation brought the professional value system more closely into line with the democratic ideal of Western society and opened the way for viewing social work as a service to which the individual has a right rather than one which is imposed upon him by society.

This development unquestionably spelled progress, for it helped to shape the image of a helping profession as a discipline based on the scientific knowledge of human behavior and existing independent of the institutions of charity and social control. At the same time this formulation of professional objectives raised some new problems concerning the ability and authority of social work to give service to people who need it but appear unwilling to accept it.

Discussion around this problem has held center stage for several years now, and a recognition has gradually been gaining ground that there is need to redefine such concepts as self-determination and authority in order to make room for an extension of services to clients who do not request them or who may even reject them. At the same time the growing interest in and demand for research in social work have emphasized the need to reconsider the concept of uniqueness in respect to clients.

Uniqueness is defined here as a complex combination of traits not duplicated in some of its singular aspects of structure and function. If uniqueness were meant to imply that there were no uniformities in behavior, and therefore no basis for generalizations about societal functioning, the concept would hinder rather than promote the development of the social work profession.

Reservations about the research process of generalizing and categorizing have been most pronounced in the area of evaluating behavior. The striving of the profession to free itself from the judgmental approach can be seen as the major reason for this view. But such considerations must not stand in the way of a process which holds promise of adding essential knowledge to the development of the social work field.

From the point of view of professional process the danger of "judgmentalism" must be weighed against the need to spell out standards of evaluation for the sake of research and as a basis for sound agency practice. Evaluation is an integral part of social work practice. Case acceptance, diagnosis, treatment, supervision, termination of treatment—all these processes and others involve evaluation of some phase of clients' functioning as a basis for service planning.

However, most evaluation of treatment is done strictly on a case-by-case basis. This is a common state of affairs in the helping professions which have as their primary goal the giving of service to people who have problems. The medical practitioner confronted with a patient describing feelings of discomfort or pain is chiefly concerned with helping that person, not in testing medical theory in the way that the medical researcher does.

Though a physician treats each patient uniquely, he does so against a background of well-documented and well-tested knowledge. Diagnosis is established by a review and grouping of the patient's symptoms which are compared with previously documented patterns of pathology. Treatment is then charted on the basis of method established through scientific procedure.

By contrast, the social worker does not generally offer services on the basis of firmly established knowledge of treatment methods suitable for dealing with diverse problem situations. Instead, he copes with the situation presented by the client by a combination of processes. These include: using psychological and social theory which might help in explaining the behavior encountered; recalling instances from first-hand experience, teachers, or peers, or in the literature which deals with comparable problems; relying on his insight, skill, and personality, all of which may have yielded favorable results in the past; using the trial-and-error method in the hope that errors will be followed by positive learning; consulting with persons more expert in the problems presented; and making referral to resources more especially equipped to deal with the problems presented.

The shortcomings of a situation in which a profession needs to rely upon a "knowledge base" as diffuse and uncertain as the sources cited above are quite obvious. The Committee on Practice of the National Association of Social Workers and the Council on Social Work Education have clearly expressed the need to give priority to research and to the creation of cumulative knowledge as one of the important goals of the profession.

There is hardly an area of social work in which the need for systematic evaluation is greater than the area of service to the multi-problem family. That family has been dubbed hard-to-reach, unreachable, resistive—terms which tell as much about the way services failed to achieve their goal as they do about the family itself. Projects for helping the multi-problem family, which have sprung up all over the nation, have been built upon the premise that past services had not been geared to meet the needs of these families. These projects have generally chosen to try new service approaches. In some instances, the objective reflects a pioneer effort in relation to the total field of social work; in others, method and techniques are new to the particular community.

It would appear that any attempt to introduce new approaches, methods, or techniques in any service setting would make it absolutely mandatory to build in devices for evaluation. Any agency, institution, or community which makes a major investment in new services, it may be assumed, will wish to obtain as good an account of the efficacy of these services as can be obtained. This has unfortunately not been the case, partly because the profession has been slow to embrace the idea of research evaluation for reasons cited above, partly because such evaluation presupposes a theoretical and conceptual case for treatment which has largely been lacking.

We are proposing here that our present-day knowledge about the structure and function of the family makes it possible to set up a scheme which makes feasible evaluation of services rendered to the multi-problem family. The scheme is an outgrowth of two demonstration-research projects already noted in Chapter 1—the Family Centered Project in St. Paul, Minnesota, and the Neighborhood Improvement Project in New Haven, Connecticut. The former has been in operation since 1954 with research activities constituting a major part of its operations between 1956 and 1959; the latter got under way in the fall of 1960 using the St. Paul approach, with certain refinements made possible as a result of the analysis of St. Paul data. The following chapters, taken as a whole, indicate the beginning blueprint for evaluating efforts aimed at rehabilitating the multi-problem family.

NOTES FOR CHAPTER 2

[1] Ernest Mowrer, *Family Disorganization* (Chicago: University of Chicago Press, 1927 and 1939), p. 3.

[2] W. I. Thomas and Florian Znaniecki, *The Polish Peasant in Europe and America* (Chicago: University of Chicago Press, 1918).

[3] Ruth Shonle Cavan and Katherine Howland Ranck, *The Family and the Depression* (Chicago: University of Chicago Press, 1938).

[4] Robert Cooley Angell, *The Family Encounters the Depression* (New York: Charles Scribner's Sons, 1936).

[5] Mowrer, *op. cit.*, p. 131 and p. 143.

[6] Earl Lemon Koos, *Families in Trouble* (New York: King's Crown Press, 1946), pp. 11-12.

[7] Talcott Parsons and Robert F. Bales, *Family Socialization and Interaction Process* (Glencoe, Ill.: The Free Press, 1955).

[8] Normal W. Bell and Ezra F. Vogel, *A Modern Introduction to the Family* (Glencoe, Ill.: The Free Press, 1960).

[9] We are indebted for some of the ideas and formulations in the following paragraphs to Beverly Ayres and Joseph Lagey. See Beverly Ayres and Joseph Lagey, *A Checklist Survey of Multi-Problem Families in Vancouver City* (Vancouver, B.C.: Community Chest and Councils of the Greater Vancouver Area, 1961, mimeographed, pp. 71-78.

[10] Nathan Edward Cohen, *Social Work in the American Tradition* (New York: Dryden Press, 1958), p. 126.

[11] Albert K. Cohen, *Delinquent Boys: The Culture of the Gang* (Glencoe, Ill.: The Free Press, 1960).

[12] August B. Hollingshead and Frederick C. Redlich, *Social Class and Mental Illness: A Community Study* (New York: John Wiley & Sons, Inc., 1958).

[13] See, especially, Alexander Leighton, *My Name Is Legion* (New York: Basic Books, Inc., 1959).

[14] It is worthy of note that the National Conference of Charities and Corrections in the United States changed its name to the National Conference on Social Work only in 1917.

[15] Stuart A. Queen, *Social Work in the Light of History* (Philadelphia: J. B. Lippincott Co., 1922), p. 195.

[16] Wayne Vasey, *Government and Social Welfare* (New York: Henry Holt, 1958), p. 71.

[17] Nathan Edward Cohen, *op. cit.*, p. 19.

[18] John C. Kidneigh, "Social Work as a Profession," in *Social Work Year Book 1960* (New York: National Association of Social Workers, 1960), pp. 563-573. See p. 564.

[19] *Ibid.*, p. 564.

[20] Nathan Edward Cohen, *op. cit.*, p. 321.

[21] See Bradley Buell and Associates, *Community Planning for Human Services* (New York: Columbia University Press, 1952), pp. 1-17; *Reaching the Unreached Family* (New York: New York City Youth Board, 1958), pp. 14-28; L. L. Geismar and Beverly Ayres, *Families in Trouble* (St. Paul, Minn.: Family Centered Project, 1958).

[22] See Alice Overton and Katherine Tinker, *Casework Notebook* (St. Paul, Minn.: Family Centered Project, Greater St. Paul Community Chest and Councils, Inc., 1959).

[23] State Charities Aid Association, *"Multi-Problem Families," a New Name or a New Problem?* (New York: State Charities Aid Association, May, 1960), p. 3.

[24] *Ibid.*, p. 3.

[25] See, for instance, Nathan W. Ackerman, *The Psycho-Dynamics of Family Life* (New York: Basic Books, Inc., 1958); Otto Pollak, "A Family Diagnosis Model," *The Social Service Review,* Vol. XXXIV, No. 1, March, 1960, pp. 19-28, p. 21; Otto Pollak and Donald Brieland, "The Midwest Seminar on Family Diagnosis and Treatment," *Social Casework,* Vol. XLII, No. 7, July, 1961, pp. 319-324, p. 319; Maurice R. Friend, "The Historical Development of Family Diagnosis," *The Social Service Review,* Vol. XXXIV, No. 1, March, 1960, pp. 2-16, p. 10; Alice Voiland and associates, *Family Casework Diagnosis* (New York: Columbia University Press, 1962); Talcott Parsons and Robert Bales, *Family, Socialization and Interaction Process* (Glencoe, Ill.: The Free Press, 1955).

[26] Prominent among these are the studies carried out by the Institute of Welfare Research of the Community Service Society of New York. See, especially, J. McVicker Hunt and Leonard S. Kogan, *Measuring Results in Social Casework* (New York: Family Service Association of America, 1952); J. McVicker Hunt, Margaret Blenkner, and Leonard S. Kogan, *Testing Results in Social Casework: A Field Test of the Movement Scale* (New York: Family Service Association of America, 1950); Ann W. Shyne and Leonard S. Kogan, "A Study of Components of Movement," *Social Casework,* Vol. XXXIX, No. 6, June, 1958, pp. 332-342; see also Louis E. Pinchack and Alan W. Rollins, "A Social Adequacy Rating Scale: Preliminary Report," *Social Work,* Vol. 5, No. 2, April, 1960, pp. 71-78.

[27] Martin B. Loeb, "The Backdrop for Social Research: Theory Making and Model Building," in Leonard S. Kogan, ed., *Social Science Theory and Social Work Research* (New York: National Association of Social Workers, 1960), p. 4.

[28] "Social work is the enhancement of social functioning wherever the need for such enhancement is either socially or individually perceived." Werner W. Boehm, *Objectives of the Social Work Curriculum for the Future,* Vol. 1. *The Comprehensive Report of the Curriculum Study* (New York: Council on Social Work Education, 1959), p. 46.

[29] Mercer uses this definition to apply to the term function rather than functioning. Blaine E. Mercer, *The American Community* (New York: Random House, 1956), p. 8.

[30] Bureau of Census, Current Population Reports, *Population Characteristics,* Series P-20 (Washington, D.C.: U. S. Government Printing Office, May 19, 1948), p. 5.

[31] Talcott Parsons and Edward A. Shils, eds., *Toward a General Theory of Action* (Cambridge, Mass.: Harvard University Press, 1951), pp. 20-21, 481-496.

[32] Talcott Parsons and Robert F. Bales, *op. cit.,* p. 47.

CHAPTER

PROBLEMS OF IDENTIFICATION
AND MEASUREMENT

THE PREVALENCE OF
FAMILY DISORGANIZATION

If family disorganization or multi-problem functioning is viewed by the community or by society as social pathology the question of its prevalence must be raised. This needs to be done for two reasons:

- The scope of any process or event harmful to the welfare of man and society should be known in order that it can be dealt with by any method known to and accepted by society. Whether such action takes the form of direct treatment, legislation, or quarantine is not important in this context. What matters is that the relationship between the scope of the problem and the magnitude of the action should be known in order to permit realistic planning.

• An assessment of the effectiveness of any action also presupposes knowledge of the scope of a problem. In the long run effectiveness can be measured by whether or not the action undertaken serves to decrease, increase, or contain the phenomenon under consideration.

The availability of precise data about the prevalence of pathology is taken for granted in medicine and public health. Adequate data about social pathology are scarce because the field of social work has not developed the same expectations relative to such information. Instead, it has been reasonably satisfied with dealing with the most urgent problems and/or giving services where resources were available.

This situation has not been conducive to the growth of epidemiology, that is, the study of pathology in relation to population characteristics and processes, in the area of social problems. Existing efforts at procuring epidemiological knowledge have been handicapped by loose terminology of given phenomena. For example, some advocates of community-wide reporting in social work have dealt with the term "economic dependency" as if it were a serious disorder that needs to be eradicated. To cite another example, the term "social maladjustment" has been treated like a clearly identifiable disease such as diabetes or polio. Social work as a whole, however, has shown relatively little interest in systematic and reliable stock taking of existing welfare problems.

It is not far-fetched to suppose that the problems inherent in defining social pathology have been a hindrance to the development of social epidemiology to the same extent that the absence of an orientation aimed at pinpointing welfare problems has retarded efforts at conceptualizing community-wide pathology. In other words, one might postulate here a reciprocal relationship between orientation and knowledge rather than a one-way influence.

The pursuit of epidemiology requires, in addition to adequate conceptualization, some provision for collecting data on a community-wide basis. The two requirements unfortunately do not often go hand in hand. The most comprehensive kind of reporting usually relies on data that are readily available. Yet, the process of defining social pathology and operationalizing data collection must, of necessity, work independently of whatever information may be at hand through administrative channels. Administrative data gathering is generally very specific in terms of the requirements arising out of the operation of a given program. The process of conceptualization, by contrast, is theory related and demands data collection in keeping with the theoretical frame of reference.

The investigator who wishes to study the prevalence of a community-wide problem is faced with a dilemma: to refrain from data collection until means can be found to procure thoroughly meaningful information, or to collect data which raise questions as to their significance but are available on a community-wide basis. The decision as often as not is one of compromise between these two extremes.

The family functioning approach may, as we hope to show later, suggest a way of studying family disorganization in a meaningful manner. It is equally clear that the data required for such an analysis can be obtained only with some effort in training social workers and/or skilled interviewers in procuring and writing up such information. Short of this or an equally promising approach for gauging the scope of a community problem, certain compromise techniques may be used. An example of these techniques are two checklist studies carried out in St. Paul, Minnesota,[1] and Vancouver, British Columbia,[2] in recent years. Mention of the latter has been made in the previous chapters.

Both surveys were designed to establish the approximate number of multi-problem families in the respective communities as a basis from which to gauge the need for reaching-out services. In both studies it was agreed, for reasons of practicability, to confine the surveying to institutional channels, that is, to utilize the agencies and organizations most likely to be in contact with disorganized families. It was assumed that this approach would yield data about the bulk of multi-problem families who are in some ways dependent upon the community. In both cities the major public and private welfare agencies were canvassed. There were, however, differences in the scope of health, educational, recreational, and correctional agencies surveyed. The Vancouver canvass was broader (8,017 cases as against 4,980 in St. Paul) but did not yield a higher proportion of multi-problem cases, perhaps because the disorganized families, many of whom had multiple agency contacts, were picked up even in the St. Paul survey through at least one of the agencies serving them.

The survey technique used in both places differed only in some minor respects and was essentially as follows: All social workers giving service to families in the agencies participating in the study received instructions in completing a schedule or checklist on every one of their client families with at least one parent and one or more children under 18 in the home. The checklist, which was accompanied by instructions containing definition of terms, required the review of each case and the checking of categories appropriate to the objectives of the survey.

For purposes of both surveys, and with recognition of the limitations in the data-gathering process, a crude but operational definition of multi-problem family was decided upon. This definition was a modification of that used by Community Research Associates, Inc., in their 1948 St. Paul Family Unit Report Study.[3] A multi-problem family was defined in both the St. Paul and Vancouver surveys as one with one or more children under 18 which is characterized by (1) serious behavior disorders as evidenced by verified neglect, delinquency, mental disorders, emotional disturbance, severe conflicts in interpersonal relations, and the like; and (2) problems in one or both of the following areas: economic functioning which included continuous or intermittent relief or public assistance, excessive debts, problems around money management, and health functioning, particularly a serious health condition in adults and children.

Both studies concerned themselves with the question of reliability of reporting by comparing differences in categories checked on all cases with multiple agency contacts. Percentages of disagreement ran from 7 to 40, depending on whether information required was objective, such as family status, or whether it was more judgmental, such as behavior problems in the family. The fundamental weakness in both surveys lay in the fact that agency recording is for the most part not family centered but it focuses on programs or specific problems dealt with.

Thus, a probation officer carrying a case load of 120 may not know much about the family of orientation of one of his charges placed in an institution. Or a public assistance worker may have only the vaguest notion about the nature of the marital relationship in a family under his care.

These defects in reliability of data seriously limit their validity. As an index of family disorganization in the community, two assumptions might be made in interpreting and utilizing any survey results:

• Even if our average error in reliability runs as high as 33 per cent, our estimate about total incidence of multi-problem families in the community brings us within a sufficiently close range of the actual figure to evolve a strategy for coping with the problem.

• The chances are that the most disorganized families

were reported in the survey because these families have a tendency to become known to the social worker. The remedy for such hazardous postulating lies obviously in equipping social agencies with the tools for collecting meaningful and reliable data.

Having accepted the limitations inherent in the survey method of the St. Paul and Vancouver studies, what do they tell us about the prevalence of family disorganization?

When the total population of the two cities was used as a base, the estimated proportion of persons identified by the above-mentioned method as belonging to disorganized families was 4.5 per cent for St. Paul and 4.6 per cent for Vancouver. The figures were arrived at by counting the average multi-problem family as a six-person group, an estimate supported by preliminary studies in both communities. The estimate for multi-problem families as percentages of all families in the two communities was found to be 2.2 and 2.3, respectively.

These survey findings are not too different from those established in the 1948 Family Unit Report Study done by Community Research Associates,[4] which had covered 37,-369 families as a result of wider agency participation. The 1948 study, in contrast to the two later surveys, included a considerable number of recreation and group work agencies.[5] A total of 6,466 families, roughly 6 per cent of the families in St. Paul, were identified as multi-problem in the 1948 study.[6] The definition used was more inclusive than that used in the 1957 checklist survey and comprised some families who had no adjustment problems. Moreover, the term "family" was used in a less-restricted manner than in the two other later studies.[7]

Unfortunately the 1948 survey provided no information on the reliability of data. A subsequent analysis of the data by the Research Department of the Amherst Wilder Foundation of St. Paul in terms similar to those of the later checklist studies yielded an estimate of roughly 2 per cent of families identified as disorganized in St. Paul in 1948.

In a progress report on human welfare in New York City, a study committee reported that "at most 5 per cent of the city's families with children under 18 can be regarded as multi-problem units." [8] This ratio would be smaller if all the families in the community were used as a base for computation.

In 1960 the Neighborhood Improvement Project of New Haven, Connecticut, conducted an intensive survey of all the households, numbering 300, in a low-income public housing project, in an effort to locate every seriously disorganized family with children under 18 in the project. The survey preceded the establishment of a treatment program for these multi-problem families. Using the criteria employed in the 1948 St. Paul study, 25 families were found to be clearly multi-problem. This number is about 8 per cent of the families in this particular neighborhood, which is known for its high rates of economic dependency and delinquent behavior. Though it is not known how representative this housing project is of other deteriorated areas, it can safely be said that deprived neighborhoods contain the bulk of multi-problem families in a community.[9] This conclusion is borne out by the Vancouver survey in which eight census tracts out of a total of forty-nine were reported to have multi-problem families constituting between 3 and 6.2 per cent of all families in the area, whereas twenty other tracts had rates below 1 per cent.[10]

What do these various findings add up to? Allowing for a considerable margin of error due to low or unknown reliability in reporting, we do get converging evidence that the proportion of the most disorganized families in the urban community who are *known* to the community is relatively small, ranging perhaps between 2 and 3 per cent of all the families in the community. However, this small group receives a great many services as was shown in a study of one hundred St. Paul families by Geismar and Ayres [11] and in the findings of Bradley Buell and Associates which state that these families "were absorbing well over half of the combined services of the community's dependency, health, and adjustment agencies." [12]

We do not know whether St. Paul and Vancouver are representative with regard to the prevalence of known community disorganization. It is possible that economic and social factors accounting for demographic patterns different from those in these two cities exist elsewhere and are associated with different ratios of disorganization. This question could be answered by checklist-type surveys in a cross section of communities repeated at given time intervals, designed to study differences resulting from variations in socio-economic forces. Basic to any such effort—and this appears to be the most important lesson emanating from the checklist studies—are provisions to assure adequate reliability of reporting data. Any community which is interested in determining the prevalence of multi-problem functioning as reflected in multi-agency contacts can take certain steps to improve the reliability of reporting data.

These steps include the acceptance, by agencies participating in the survey, of a family centered focus in serving clients, the provision for continuous data collection on family functioning, and some in-service training of social workers in the method of data gathering. An ongoing reporting operation built into agency practice is likely to yield more reliable data because it permits the establishment of a consistent focus and the development of reporting skills. Such a focus geared to a ready perception of breakdown in the psychosocial functioning of a family would hardly appear to be at odds with the basic goals of social work endorsed by most agencies.

The checklist type of survey technique for identifying

multi-problem families is based upon the assumption that the great bulk of them can be located by a review of agency case loads. Multi-problem families are thought to be "known" to the community because their disordered behavior brings them to the attention of agencies and authorities concerned with economic, health, adjustment, and correctional functions.

The study by Geismer and Ayres of one hundred St. Paul families diagnosed as seriously disorganized revealed, indeed, that these families were known not to one but to many agencies in the community. The median number of registrations during the family life cycle was thirteen, and the families had received services from nine *different* agencies, on the average. The mean number of years during which the families were known to the agencies was fifteen.[13]

This pattern of multiple registration was not surprising because it had served as the means by which identification and selection for treatment was carried out. Therefore it would be accurate to state that families known to many agencies tend to be multi-problem in functioning. The converse may be true, but we are not aware of any comprehensive studies which have investigated this relationship. To do so it would be necessary to study the social functioning of a cross section of a given population and relate malfunctioning to the agency registration pattern.

Little is known regarding the prevalence of family disorganization in middle-class families, although the records of any therapist or mental health clinic will show that multiproblem behavior in the middle and upper strata of society is not an isolated phenomenon. Families in the higher socioeconomic groups differ significantly from those in the lower ones by their ability to shield problem behavior from the community at large by the purchase of services which are private and confidential in nature. It is no accident that the increased use of public family counseling services by middle-class clients coincided with a tendency by those agencies to discontinue registering clients with the community social service exchange [14] or to register "selectively." Selectivity generally means omitting from the list of names transmitted to the exchange those clients who request "maximum" confidentiality in treatment or who are given confidential handling because the agency considers it appropriate.

The timing and rate at which multi-problem families establish service contacts with agencies in the community is of interest to the planners and administrators of welfare services. As an offshoot of the Geismar and Ayres study noted above, Ayres, while she was research analyst for the St. Paul Family Centered Project, studied the agency registrations of one hundred disorganized families who were then receiving treatment.[15] The study was based on a tabulation of the Central Registration Bureau (Social Service Exchange) data and comprised information about contacts of families as well as contacts of the parents or heads of these families with local agencies. Since only a few families had moved into Minnesota after marriage, and since data from the other major exchanges in the state were included in the study, the Ayres analysis gives a fairly comprehensive picture of the families' history of agency contacts. The study included all the major agencies giving various forms of public assistance, adjustment services, and free health services.

Twenty-four per cent of the families studied were active with one or more agencies at the time of marriage or made their first contact within one month after marriage, 39 per cent were known within six months, 51 per cent within one year, 78 per cent within six years, and 88 per cent within eight years. The bulk (57 per cent) of the first registrations were with agencies giving public assistance, 25 per cent were with adjustment services, and 18 per cent with health agencies.[16]

In a study of a sample of fifteen disorganized families in

New Haven, Connecticut, 64 per cent of the families had their first agency contact within fifteen months after marriage; in a control group of more stable families in the same socio-economic class only 33 per cent of the families had such contact during that time period.[17]

Of the one hundred St. Paul families, there were only seventeen in which no relative of either man or woman was known to the Central Registration Bureau.[18] The parents of both the man and the woman were known in 41 per cent of the families, the parents of either were known in 37 per cent, whereas *only* other relatives (siblings) of man or woman had registrations with the exchange in 5 per cent of the cases.[19] (In the New Haven study, 25 per cent of the disorganized families had no registration on the parents of the family heads.)

Conversely, Ayres' analysis showed that in 72 per cent of all families in which there was a child over twenty (33 families), one or more of the children had become known to local social agencies through separate registration as families or individuals. This registration involved 52 per cent of these children who were twenty years or older, 62 per cent of those above age twenty-four, 68 per cent of those above age twenty-nine, and 80 per cent of those who were thirty-two or older. The hundred families had only six sons or daughters aged thirty-five and over, but all these were known to the Central Registration Bureau.

No analysis was made in the Geismar and Ayres study of the relative frequency of registrations over the years following marriage. However, the impression was gained that the number of registrations increased with the age and co-extensively with the size of the family, since these families had an average of 5.8 children born at minimal intervals starting before or shortly after marriage. The registration pattern of fifteen disorganized families in New Haven showed a positively accelerating curve, that is, registrations tended to increase as years after marriage increased. It is of interest that the control group (in the same socio-economic class) of more stable families showed a negatively accelerating curve on agency registrations.[20]

Several tentative conclusions emerge from the statistics given above. The bulk of multi-problem families who can be identified through agency registrations becomes known to the community within a short time after marriage. The Geismar and Ayres study produced evidence that shortness of the time span between marriage and the first application for agency help (usually Public Assistance) is directly correlated with severity of family disorganization several years later.[21] The connection between these two factors is hypothetical but might involve lack of motivation resulting from deficiency in ego structure or from cultural conditioning in the home, both of which might explain the young parents' rush to obtain agency support after marriage and their inability to keep the family from going to pieces at a later date.

The supposition that hasty application for agency help is related to the home situation received support from the Ayres study of one hundred St. Paul multi-problem families.[22] Heads of families whose own parents were known to the Central Registration Bureau were more likely to apply for agency help within one year after marriage than family heads whose parents were not known. The percentages for those receiving agency service within twelve months of marriage, according to their own parents' contacts with social agencies were as follows: where both parents were known, 57 per cent had received services; where one parent was known, 51 per cent had received services; and where no parent was known, only 9 per cent had received agency services within one year after marriage. A substantial minority of families (about one-fourth of the families in the Ayres study) do not come to the attention of the community until six years after the founding of the family. During that time they manage without financial assistance, do not come into conflict with the law, and otherwise do not show any extreme behavior problems which would bring them to the attention of a social agency. The parents of these families were in most instances not known to the Central Registration Bureau. Out of 33 St. Paul client families who applied for help seven years or more after marriage, 19 had neither set of parents known, 10 had one set of parents known, and only 4 had both sets of parents known to the Central Registration Bureau. These figures contrast sharply with those cited above for the group of families who applied for help within one year of marriage. Only 9 per cent of these were children of parents who were never known to the Central Registration Bureau.[23]

The historical pattern of agency contacts cited from all St. Paul data points to a long-standing condition of disorganization for most of the multi-problem families. This observation is of potential interest for any inquiry into etiology.

A PERSPECTIVE FOR ASSESSING FAMILY FUNCTIONING

Effective assessment of family or social functioning must rest upon clear definitions of the kind of behavior that is to be assessed. As suggested in Chapter 2, this may be done by viewing the family not merely as an aggregate of individuals but also as an interacting group of persons playing mutually complementary roles and carrying out certain basic tasks or functions which are necessary for the welfare of the family and are in keeping with the expectations of society. In Chapter 2, family functioning was presented in a broad theoretical frame of reference. Our purpose here is to consider family functioning in terms that are useful in assessing it.

This approach suggests that we examine the roles which

each person is playing and ask whether they contribute to his own and his family's well-being, whether they are in line with his potential for social functioning, and whether they are in keeping with societal expectations. Moreover, we must consider to what extent those tasks which can be identified as family functions are being performed in a manner which is conducive to the welfare of the family as well as the community.

The Family Centered Project of St. Paul developed a model for assessing family functioning of disorganized families.[24] This model was named the Profile of Family Functioning. The Profile is a chart of a family's social functioning in nine categories or areas and 26 subcategories on a seven-point continuum ranging from adequate to inadequate behavior. Data for the chart are collected by means of open-ended interviews with family members and reading of agency records pertaining to the family's functioning. The narrative information, after being entered in the Profile schedule under their appropriate categories and subcategories, is rated by two or more judges on the seven-point continuum mentioned above.

The Profile of Family Functioning was tested for reliability and applied in the study of 150 St. Paul families who had received family centered treatment.[25] The Profile has also been used in the Neighborhood Improvement Project of New Haven, Connecticut, the Research Demonstration Project with Dependent Multi-Problem Families of Elmira, New York, and several other research action programs. Since the details of this particular method of analyzing the functioning of problem families were presented in several publications, we shall review here only its conceptual underpinnings and sketch its basic outline.

Individual Behavior and Adjustment

In presenting the two aspects of family functioning in Chapter 2, we inquired first into the nature of each individual's functioning. We term this category of observations "Individual Behavior and Adjustment." It comprises each family member's personality structure, which includes his physical appearance, attitudes, and behavior, and also pathological characteristics of a physiological, psychological, and social nature. Examples of the latter are physical and mental handicaps, anxieties, pathogenic conflicts, and character disorders.

The second aspect of the category "Individual Behavior and Adjustment" covers sets of roles which family members play in daily life. Typical roles include those of husband, wife, parent, homemaker, breadwinner, child, sibling, student, member of peer group, member of an organization. Since every member of a family plays a great number of roles both inside and outside the family, assessment takes into account how well these roles are being performed and integrated within the personality structure of each family member. Integration refers to the compatibility and complementarity of roles which may either permit the individual to function in keeping with the expectations of the group and enjoy good mental health, or may make him experience conflict between roles or between roles and expectations and may affect his personality adversely.

Areas of Social Functioning Involving Role
Performance in the Family Group

As stated earlier, an area of social functioning represents a concept that groups together all those sets of activities or roles performed by family members with the aim of getting a certain job done. The primary concern in appraising the convergence of roles by areas is how well the tasks are performed rather than who performs them. One group of areas involves role playing within the primary social system called family. This means that contacts, whether of an expressive or of an instrumental nature, are with members of the family only.

Three areas represent functioning in such intrafamilial roles. The first is termed *Family Relationships and Unity*.[26] It comprises the subareas of "marital relationship," "relationships between parents and children," "relationships among children," and "family solidarity" or family cohesiveness, as indicated by likeness or difference in values, beliefs, and goals among family members. The second area of intrafamilial functioning is termed *Care and Training of Children*, which includes physical care and training methods. The latter includes data covering such questions as these: how do parents think children should behave, how and by whom is approval shown, how are limits set and enforced, are parents consistent in training and discipline and do they work together. The third area covers *Home Conditions and Household Practices*. Information is sought regarding the neighborhood, physical facilities, including the condition of the home; household equipment; accommodations for sleeping, bathing, cooking; housekeeping standards, which refers to the way the household is managed; the nature of the diet enjoyed by the family; and related subjects.

Areas of Social Functioning Involving Roles Both Within and Outside the Family Group

One area in this group is *Social Activities*, comprising role playing by family members both within and outside the family system. The subcategory "informal associations" refers to social and recreational activities with members of the immediate or extended family, social contacts with friends and neighbors. It calls for information on the question, "What does the family do together, or what do its members do separately during their leisure time; what do they do to have fun?" The subcategory "formal associations" inquires into the participation of family members in more structured activities such as church, clubs, neighborhood centers, unions, PTA's. It has been our observation that the area of Social Activities is neglected in the records of caseworkers. A possible reason for this might be found in the fact that social work, because of its problem orientation, has shown concern mainly for the negatives or weaknesses in psychological and social behavior and has underemphasized the positives or strengths in social functioning.

The area of *Economic Practices* likewise calls for role performance both within and outside the family. The latter is represented by the subarea "source and amount of family income" which covers such questions as these: where is the money coming from, is it adequate for the needs of the family, what is the job situation of the main income provider. The subarea "job situation" calls for information on the nature of work, job satisfaction, irritants and frustrations at work. Functioning within the family is represented by the third subarea entitled "use of money" which calls for answers on how well money is managed, who controls the purse, priorities in spending money, amount of debts, and the like.

Another "mixed" area with regard to roles played in and outside the family is *Health Conditions and Practices*. The subarea "health problems" covers information on the health of the family members, whereas the subarea "health practices" seeks information as to how health problems are being met and how the family protects the health of the family members. This covers functioning within the family, such as activities to improve the health of sick members in the home or to assure good health and prevent illness of those who are well. "Health practices" also pertains to the use of resources in the community for both curative purposes and the prevention of illness.

Areas of Social Functioning Involving
Role Performance Outside the Family

Social functioning involving role performance largely beyond the family group covers the area *Use of Community Resources* which deals with the way the family sees and uses the school, the church, health resources, social agencies, and recreational agencies. It also covers the area *Relationship to the Social Worker,* of special relevance to the multi-problem family in treatment, since the relationship to the worker and the family's use of the worker may be seen to reflect in some measure the way its members relate to the community and are able to use help in resolving their problems.

Areas of Family Functioning Involving Social
Relationships or Instrumental Goals

A further distinction can be made between family functioning characterized by social relationships and functioning in which such relationships are subordinated to the attainment of instrumental goals. The expressive-instrumental dichotomy discussed in the previous chapter does not clearly differentiate among the areas of family functioning.

All functioning involving social relationships has expressive components, but relationship areas such as *Care and Training of Children* and *Use of Community Resources* are to a large extent also instrumentally oriented. A two-way categorization stressing the predominance of social relationships or their subordination to instrumental goals is therefore more appropriate for handling the data with which we are concerned. By placing this categorization against the intrafamilial-extrafamilial categorization described above we obtain the schemata given below. The eight areas of family functioning in the schemata plus the category *Individual Behavior and Adjustment* are the basic working tools in the studies reported here. It should be noted that the category *Individual Behavior and Adjustment* must of necessity be viewed separately from the fourfold conceptualization shown in the schemata since the functioning of an individual in a family generally combines more than one type and often all four types of functioning in the roles he plays.

SCHEMATA OF FAMILY FUNCTIONING

	Functioning That Is Largely Intra-familial	*Functioning That Is Largely Extra-familial or Mixed*
Functioning Characterized by Social Relationships	Family Relationships and Unity Care and Training of Children	Social Activities Use of Community Resources Relationship to Social Worker
Functioning in Which Social Relationships are Subordinated to the Attainment of Instrumental Goals	Home Conditions and Household Practices	Economic Practices Health Conditions and Practices

It should be remembered that the organization of areas for the Profile of Family Functioning has been specially geared to the multi-problem family which is generally in the lower socio-economic stratum of society. This is to say that in describing conceptually the functioning of any other type of family in our society, the organization of the Profile might have to be changed in relation to the degree of prominence of certain types of functioning in the total behavior pattern of family members. For instance, in describing middle-class family functioning, political and religious functioning might be covered under main rather than subcategories, and relationship to the social worker might not merit the important focus assigned to it in our scheme.

Following our effort to outline areas of social functioning, we are now faced with the task of evaluating given patterns of behavior which have been sketched in terms of the profile scheme suggested here. Evaluation requires standards with which to compare the functioning of the families studied. In the previous chapter we discussed the need for evaluation in social work and pointed up some obstacles in the way of having the principle of evaluation accepted by the profession. The view has been expressed that the growing interest in research has given impetus to efforts at evaluation of client functioning. Indeed, special interest on the part of practitioners has been aroused to the extent that evaluative methods have come to show some relevance to treatment.

The Family Centered Project of St. Paul devoted a major part of its research effort to developing a scheme of levels of functioning which could serve as a model against which to compare the functioning of multi-problem families. This scheme had been tested in a reliability study [27] and was used for assessing family functioning in St. Paul and the Neighborhood Improvement Project of New Haven, Connecticut.

Without going into the details of the evaluation method, it is pertinent to recapitulate briefly the rationale for the levels of functioning approach. In view of the fact that social welfare in general and social work in particular are constantly impelled, for purposes of treatment, to evaluate clients and client families on the basis of what the profession views as acceptable behavior, an evaluation of groups of families can hardly be considered a departure from professional practice. Nevertheless, we need to be mindful of the risk inherent in applying standards which reflect norms of behavior of a status group higher than the one to which the family whose functioning we are evaluating belongs.

To avoid doing this, the standards or levels of functioning selected must not be so narrowly circumscribed as to constitute prescriptions for class behavior. A model for evaluation should, in fact, set up base lines against which behavior can be judged to be seriously at odds with the law and inimical to the welfare of the family and community, or in line with broad expectations of the status group and conducive to the welfare of the family and community. The intent is obviously to define levels which are broad enough to meet the latter specifications.

A definition of minimum levels of social functioning is actually implicit in all social work with seriously disorganized families. The granting of public assistance, the filing of neglect petitions, the placement of children, and the other decisions carried out by the social worker, all require a judgment as to whether or not functioning in one or more areas is at a level at which intervention by the community is in order. Protective services are rendered whenever an assessment of the family situation suggests that the family is unable without professional help to provide the minimum standards of child care for their offspring.

The concept chosen here for defining levels of functioning is one suggested by the discussion above. It may be most appropriately termed community concern. It pertains to the success or failure of the family group to function in such a way as to ensure the welfare of its own members or those of the community around it. Community concern may be aroused by the impairment of, or threat to, the well-being of family members, especially the children. This might take the form of socially and psychologically deviant behavior on the part of parents and/or children. Community concern may also result because of serious problems in physical and mental health, economic performance, family relationships, and other areas of family functioning.

A second facet of community concern is behavior which adversely affects the welfare of the community. In its most extreme form this means the violation of laws designed to protect the community. Less easily definable but of some importance as a factor of community concern is the extent to which the family has been violating mores which are part of the basic value system, for example, not toilet training children until after the usual ages, or failing to permit them to join peer groups.

A joint effort by researchers and caseworkers in the St. Paul Family Centered Project resulted in the Levels of Social Functioning scheme which is reproduced with slight modifications in the Appendix of this book. The general criteria for evaluation of family functioning upon three levels—inadequate, marginal, and adequate functioning—which were used as anchor points of a seven-point scale in the evaluation studies, are as follows: [28]

Inadequate Functioning (Community has a right to intervene.) Laws and/or mores clearly violated. Behavior of family members a threat to the community. Family life characterized by extreme conflict, neglect, severe deprivation or very poor relationships resulting in physical and/or emotional suffering of family members; disruption of family life imminent, children in clear and present danger because of conditions above or other behavior inimical to their welfare.

Marginal Functioning (Behavior not sufficiently harmful to justify intervention.) No violation of major laws although behavior of family members is contrary to what is acceptable for status group. Family life marked by conflict, apathy, or unstable relationships which are a potential threat to welfare of family members and community; each crisis poses the danger of family's disruption, but children are not in imminent danger.

Adequate Functioning (Behavior in line with community expectations.) Laws and mores are observed; behavior is acceptable to status group. Family life is stable, members have a sense of belonging, family is able to handle problems without facing disruption, children are being raised in an atmosphere conducive to healthy physical and emotional development. Socialization process carried out affirmatively; adequate training in social skills.

These criteria, when they are broken down into their components corresponding to the profile areas of family functioning (see Appendix), provide a guide line for evaluating the functioning of disorganized families. Although the Levels of Functioning scheme provides a structure for facilitating classification and subsequent measurement, it does rely upon the judgment of those charged with processing the data. Within this structure, as has been shown in the St. Paul Manual,[29] fairly reliable judgments may be obtained. At the same time, the flexible character of the scheme and the need to have it adapted to different settings and population groups must be strongly emphasized.

TESTING THE CONCEPTUAL FRAMEWORK

The test of a conceptual framework is its capacity for ordering actual data in a manner which permits meaningful description, further analysis, and interpretation relative to the formulation of theory. The St. Paul Profile of Family Functioning was tested initially on 150 seriously disorganized families who had been receiving family centered services in a project established by a group of agencies to extend such services on a community-wide basis.

The criteria for selecting the 150 families insured that they were among the most problematic in the community. Families were initially selected by the participating agencies on the basis of being hard to reach and as not having, in the past, responded to treatment. These families were then screened by an interagency committee. Acceptance as a Family Centered Project case was based on the existence of serious problems in the behavior area and in the areas of health and/or economic functioning, as well as the presence of one or more children under 18 who could be classified as being in "clear and present danger." This represented a condition in which the immediate physical and/or emotional welfare of the child was threatened to the extent that the community had a clear-cut responsibility to step in.

The application of the Profile of Family Functioning to this group of disorganized families has several purposes. It reveals the nature of functioning and malfunctioning in terms of nine categories of family functioning. Since each category is evaluated on the same basic dimension, the analysis will show whether severe disorganization implies malfunctioning across the board or more serious problem functioning in some areas than in others. Statistical manipulation by means of a technique called scale analysis will disclose whether the pattern of functioning characteristic for the group also holds true for the individual family.

Further uses of the application of the Profile include a quantitative comparison of the 150 St. Paul multi-problem families with groups of families similarly identified as disorganized and with other family groups known to differ in their social functioning. Such a comparison comes under the heading of testing the instrument for validity. Validity provides evidence of the extent to which a particular measure, in this case the Profile, differentiates among families in ways that are comparable to other accepted criteria, such as broad diagnostic information which agencies have about their clients.

Before looking at the patterns of functioning proper, brief reference should be made to the mechanics of assessing family functioning in this project. The nature of social functioning of each family was documented by a social worker who served the family by means of the open-ended Profile Schedule. The narrative was then rated by two judges.[30] The system of documenting functioning and rating it had previously been subjected to reliability tests.[31] Ratings for each family were then entered on a Profile chart which showed nine category scores. Subsequently, the means of area scores for all the 150 families were computed.

Keeping in mind the scale of values on which families are being rated (see previous section in this chapter), ranging from Inadequate (1) through Marginal (4) to Adequate (7) family functioning, the following mean-score distribution and Profile obtains for the 150 St. Paul families.

The array of categories of family functioning shown in Figure 1 represents a scale [32] in the sense in which Guttman and others define the term.[33] Guttman means by scale a "unidimensional" continuum on which respondents can be ranked according to their patterns of responses on several scale items. More concretely, in the case of the 150 disorganized families, the discovery of scalability indicates a uniformity of functioning pattern for the individual family which follows rather closely the Profile of mean scores shown in Figure 1. Thus, allowing for some deviations from the statistical model within the range of the criteria of functioning, most of the families in this group functioned least adequately in the areas of the top of the Profile, somewhat more adequately in the middle categories, and relatively most adequately in the bottom categories.

Another way of stating this is as follows: The multi-problem family in this research project shows a characteristic pattern of functioning or malfunctioning, not a random pattern. Knowing the total functioning score of any single family permits one to conclude with some accuracy where social functioning is relatively high and where it is relatively low. Because of the existence of such a characteristic interrelationship in degrees of malfunctioning among the nine categories we are able to speak of a unidimensional continuum called family functioning.

FIGURE 1: PROFILE OF FAMILY FUNCTIONING BASED ON MEAN SCORES FOR
150 DISORGANIZED FAMILIES—LEVEL OF FAMILY FUNCTIONING *

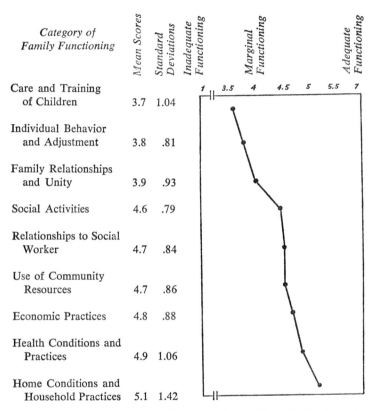

Category of Family Functioning	Mean Scores	Standard Deviations
Care and Training of Children	3.7	1.04
Individual Behavior and Adjustment	3.8	.81
Family Relationships and Unity	3.9	.93
Social Activities	4.6	.79
Relationships to Social Worker	4.7	.84
Use of Community Resources	4.7	.86
Economic Practices	4.8	.88
Health Conditions and Practices	4.9	1.06
Home Conditions and Household Practices	5.1	1.42

* The order of categories in the figure above differs slightly from the order derived from scalogramming this population. In the latter technique Social Activities followed rather than preceded *Relationship to Social Worker* and *Use of Community Resources*. In scale ordering, scores were dichotomized (marginal and below versus above marginal), whereas here the means of the seven-point scores were used.

Let us now look at the categories themselves and the meaning of their distribution for the families studied. Least adequate role performance is found in areas characterized by expressive behavior. Such role playing is, of course, part of

Individual Behavior and Adjustment which was defined as the sum total of individual roles played by each member, but here expressive and instrumental forms of functioning are joined in the individual personality. Expressive components may be seen as dominant in the other two areas of least adequate functioning, *Care and Training of Children* and *Family Relationships and Unity.* In both these areas there is a major emphasis upon the integration of roles in the family system and upon the social and emotional satisfaction of family members.

In the next three areas of relatively lesser inadequacy the expressive component in behavior is perhaps overshadowed by instrumental goals of maintaining the family system in relation to the larger environment, particularly neighborhood and community. This is most true of *Relationship to Social Worker* and *Use of Community Resources.* In *Social Activities* there is a more even balancing between expressive and instrumental components of behavior.

The relatively most adequate areas of family functioning, *Economic Practices, Health Conditions and Practices* and *Home and Household Practices* are predominantly instrumental in nature. They represent role performances where the focus is upon maintaining the family as a physical and economic unit in society by means of providing an income, preserving the health of its members, and keeping them sheltered.

The dividing line between expressive and instrumental functioning is not clear cut. This is at least partly due to the fact that the scale categories themselves do not represent pure entities in terms of this conceptual differentiation. A more cogent differentiation in area groupings is found by distinguishing among categories comprising intrafamilial relationships, extrafamilial relationships, and instrumental functioning.

Disregarding for purposes of this analysis the area *Indi-*

vidual Behavior and Adjustment which is a composite of relationship and instrumental roles, we find that the two categories rated as below marginal in adequacy—*Care and Training of Children* and *Family Relationships and Unity*— comprise sets of behavior involving intrafamilial relationships. Substantially greater competence is shown by the disorganized families in functioning involving social relations with individuals, groups, organizations, agencies, and institutions outside the family group in the categories *Social Activities, Relationship to Social Worker* and *Use of Community Resources.* The levels of performance here are at a similar level, clearly above the marginal co-ordinate. Standard deviations, reflecting the scatter of cases to both sides of the mean position, suggest, of course, that the community relations of some families are problematic enough to justify professional intervention. Furthermore, by the standards of functioning laid out in the previous section, ratings between 4 and 5 do not denote stable or problem-free functioning. On the contrary, they denote in the present context a limited relatedness to neighborhood and community, a lack of formal as well as informal social activities, a general failure to make use of community resources. Relationships to the community are restricted, not seriously discordant or antagonistic. We shall take a closer look at this as well as other aspects of family functioning in the following chapter.

It is worthy of note that in the multi-problem family relationships outside the family are less problematic than intrafamilial relationships. This observation is not entirely surprising. The same mechanism appears to be at play here as in the more normal family. In our society people have a stake in keeping their problems under cover since the larger community shows lack of understanding and sympathy for those who are problem ridden. Displaying one's lack of interpersonal competence or projecting its consequences toward the community can lead to further loss of income, respect, friends, and so on beyond the damage already suffered as a result of an unstable or unhappy home.

A further explanation of the lesser adequacy in intra-familial relationships might be seen in the fact that they constitute a more rigorous test of interpersonal competence than the more loosely structured relationships to friends, neighbors, and agencies. The relative absence of such competence would seem to be more productive of tension, dissatisfaction, alienation, and the like in the home situation than in the community.

The three categories of relatively greatest adequacy— *Economic Practices, Health Conditions and Practices,* and *Home Conditions and Household Practices*—represent a joining of instrumental roles. These denote behavior with reference to concrete activities such as making a living, looking after the health of family members, and running the household. The levels of performance here, too, were only one scale step removed from the marginal co-ordinate, indicating functioning that is potentially problematic for many of the families studied and actually problematic for some of them. Yet, instrumental sets of behavior exceed in adequacy all functioning characterized mainly by interpersonal relationships.

Looking now at the total profile of the 150 St. Paul multi-problem families who were identified by the community as seriously disorganized on the basis of definite criteria, as stated above, the following conclusions emerge:

• Multi-problem behavior thus identified takes the form of family functioning which can be located closely below and above the marginal position by the scale of values spelled out above.

• Marginal functioning denotes behavior that is potentially threatening to the welfare of the family and the community.

• The families show most disorganization and greatest

instability in the area of interpersonal relationships, especially among family members.

• They reveal somewhat greater adequacy in the physical maintenance of the family group.

The last point deserves some elaboration in view of the fact that so much is being written about the problems of ill health and economic dependency of the multi-problem families. The existence of these problems is a matter of record in every major urban community.[34] Yet, despite the proliferation of these problems, the multi-problem family functions as a family, at least in a physical sense. One or two parents or parent-substitutes live together in a household with one or more dependent children whose minimal physical needs for food and shelter are being met. Judging by our Profile they are met somewhat better than the social and emotional needs of children and parents.

As a result, we have a social group whose mainstay is its structure and physical functioning. As long as family members stay together and have their physical requirements attended to we are able to acknowledge the existence of a family. Interpersonal relationship patterns scarcely meet, and in many cases completely fail to meet the needs of family members. Such a situation is reflected in a high rate of marital conflict, absent fathers, neglect of children, alcoholism, delinquency, and other forms of deviant behavior.[35] The multi-problem family may, therefore, be said to be a kinship group whose structure is seriously weakened by precarious social functioning.

Up to this point we have examined the characteristics of the profile of the multi-problem family. Evidence of reliability or consistency in yielding measurements of the instrument is cited in the manual, *Measuring Family Functioning*.[36] Subsequent use of the Profile with various groups of client population has revealed consistently satisfactory reliability.[37] The question of validity of the scale, or its ability to measure what it is designed to measure, has received scant attention so far.

The validity of the family functioning scale or that of any other tool of psychosocial measurement may be defined as the extent to which differences in scores reflect true differences among individuals, groups, or situations in the characteristic which the scale or other tool seeks to measure.[38] Two types of validity may be considered, construct validity and external validity.

Construct validity pertains to the theoretical or conceptual appropriateness of the instrument. In this instance, it may be asked whether the categories and anchor points for measurement on the scale correspond to standards of professional service. An affirmative answer to this question would seem justified in view of the fact that the tool of measurement was developed as a collaborative project between casework and research in the St. Paul Family Centered Project.

As already noted, the Profile of Family Functioning evolved from the diagnostic interview schedule used by the caseworkers in the St. Paul Project. The system of ratings was tested initially, informally, against independent judgments of caseworkers in order to establish whether the rating method corresponded to criteria applied by practitioners. Eventually, the casework processes of screening in, yearly evaluations, and decisions on closing the case came to be reported in what on the surface appear to be research terms. Thus, a case might be accepted in the Project because family functioning was seen as of concern or as submarginal in the areas of Family Relationships, Child Care, Health Practices, and Economic Practices; or a case might be closed because of positive movement in three or more areas, thus making functioning above marginal in nearly all categories. The acceptance of such research terminology meant essentially that the caseworkers found it convenient and appropriate to use concepts of measurement for giving a diagnostic evaluation of a particular client family.

External validity, the second type to be considered, calls for establishing the correspondence between the scores of measurement produced by an instrument and observable differences on an independent criterion of the property being measured. Such criteria are hard to come by in the case of properties based upon abstract concepts such as family functioning. However, an approximation to a criterion representing close identity with this property can be found by selecting client families from several social work settings whose client populations are known to differ from one setting to another. Comparison of profiles of client groups with known population characteristics in diverse settings does not provide a rigorous test. However, information about clients' problems and their general social situation provides an indication of the character of their functioning. Differences inferred relate to their general level of family functioning and to the concentration of problems in certain areas. This is shown by the type of services agencies render.

Let us consider three client populations in addition to the 150 St. Paul families in an effort to provide evidence of external validity of the Profile of Family functioning. The following groups are selected:

• A group of 36 multi-problem families, in order to establish whether the Profiles for families known to be disorganized are similar in character.

• A random sample of 70 families receiving Aid to Dependent Children (ADC), because of a partial or complete lack of a family income. These families were not seen as being particularly problematic in other areas. No member of the seventy families was involved with law enforcement authorities at the time of the study and no neglect petitions on children were pending.

• A random sample of 30 families receiving casework

services from a private family service. Problems dealt with involved chiefly marital relationships and to a lesser extent parent-child relations and behavior disorders of children. This population represented a higher status group than the other two groups.

A decision on testing the Profiles requires a prediction on their location and shape on the Levels of Functioning grid represented by seven levels of performance and nine categories of functioning. The chief distinction applies to the general level of adequacy versus inadequacy of the Profile representing each group. A secondary distinction concerns the slope of the graph showing areas of pronounced malfunctioning.

An application of the scale of family functioning to diverse client groups had revealed basic similarities among all the Profiles with regard to the slope of the graph.[39] More specifically, it was found that most families (including the multi-problem families) of various status groups served by different types of agencies evidenced relatively greatest adequacy in instrumental behavior and least adequacy in intrafamilial relationships, whereas the areas denoting relationships to the community occupied an intermediate position. The similarity therefore pertains mainly to *direction* of the graphs and not to their positions on the grid or to the nature of their slope. In other words, a prediction on the nature of family functioning should be related specifically to the magnitude of malfunctioning or well-functioning on the whole and in particular areas of each group of client families.

A prediction is made of similarity in functioning between the 150 multi-problem families discussed earlier and the 36 multi-problem families selected as a validating population. The same criteria for selection (see above) were used for both groups. In contrast to the 150 St. Paul families, the 36 cases were chosen from a New Haven low-cost public housing project comprising 300 households. A careful screening of all families with dependent children in the housing project yielded about 25 families which could be described as seriously disorganized.[40] Additional cases selected for treatment to make up the group of 36 receiving casework services were found to present less serious intrafamilial relationship problems than the original treatment group of St. Paul families. Anticipated similarities might thus be modified by somewhat greater adequacy in social functioning of the New Haven families, especially in the intrafamilial areas. Functioning in the area of *Household Conditions and Practices* should also reveal more adequate ratings for the New Haven families because of the better physical conditions attendant upon residence in the housing development. Only 20 per cent of the 150 St. Paul cases resided in housing projects.

Substantially greater adequacy in social functioning can be predicted for the two other populations: the families receiving Aid to Dependent Children and those receiving casework services from the private family agency. The latter group is expected to reveal less adequate behavior in *Family Relationships and Unity* and in *Individual Behavior and Adjustment,* since these are areas in which the families had manifested major problems calling for agency intervention. Instrumental areas of behavior, by contrast, are seen as showing greater adequacy for the family service clients because of their more secure family status.

Let us now look at the Profiles for the four client groups in order to see how they stand up in relation to the predictions made. Figure 2 shows the graphs for the four client groups, together with the mean scores of family functioning. Table 1 gives the mean scores and standard deviations for each category of family functioning.

The Profiles for the two multi-problem populations show similar mean scores (St. Paul families 4.5, New Haven families 4.6), as predicted. Indeed, the slopes of the graphs are roughly comparable, with the New Haven group showing somewhat greater adequacy in the intrafamilial area and in *Household Conditions and Practices*. Furthermore, this group, comprising housing project families, gives evidence of less problematic functioning in two relationship areas denoting interaction with the community, *Social Activities* and *Use of Community Resources*. Lesser adequacy characterizes their performance of instrumental roles with reference to providing an income and maintaining the health of family members. Except for *Care and Training of Children*, the differences in category mean scores are less than half a scale step, and the mean profile scores for the two groups are only one-tenth of a scale step apart. In short, as expected, the two Profiles for the multi-problem client populations are similar in level of functioning, and differences which emerged in several of the areas were predictable on the basis of information relative to the selection process.

Considerably higher mean functioning marks the social-role performance of the ADC families and the clients served by the family agency. The latter group, as anticipated, shows least adequacy in intrafamilial relationships which were the focus of treatment. The magnitude of such inadequacy is quite surprising and could not be predicted, although a recent review of this agency's case load by a consultant had stressed the extensive pathology found among cases treated by the agency. Although it is not the subject of the present analysis, this finding brings to the fore a point of great interest to the planner of welfare services, namely, that the multi-problem family, it seems, has no monopoly on serious malfunctioning in family relationships.

Higher status families whose extrafamilial and instrumental functioning may be comparatively adequate are likely to manifest as much as or more pathology in marital and parent-child relationships than the most disorganized families known to the community. The higher-status clients are functioning slightly better in *Household and Health Practices* but not in *Economic Practices*. If the latter finding seems surprising, in view of the limited financial means of the ADC family, it must be pointed out that the category *Economic Practices* represents a judgment not merely of the total financial resources available but also of the manner in which a family manages these resources. By and large, ADC families, because of close agency supervision, show greater aptitude in managing their budget than the higher-status families; many of the latter had incurred substantial debts and encountered real difficulty in getting along on comparatively adequate incomes.

The previous prediction about differences in functioning based on knowledge of types of client families is borne out by the differences found in mean scores of family functioning and in the Profiles placed on the social functioning grid. Differences between ADC and St. Paul multi-problem families were statistically significant.[41]

Further evidence of external validity of the scale is provided in a study done at the University of Minnesota's School of Social Work.[42] Scores on the scale of family functioning were found to differentiate clearly between a sample of multi-problem families for whom a neglect petition had been filed and a random sample of such cases not charged with the neglect of children. Low scoring on the scale was found to be directly related to a situation where action had been taken by the community to bring neglect charges against the family.[43] Finally, a comparison of Profiles based on the independent interviews of husbands and wives in ten New Jersey families showed that the marriage partners described family functioning in similar terms. Main category scores were identical on 58.8% and one scale step apart on 33.7% of the ratings. The scores differed by more than one scale step in only 7.5% of the responses.[44]

We have presented here some evidence that the Profile of

FIGURE 2: PROFILES OF FAMILY FUNCTIONING BASED ON MEAN SCORES FOR
FOUR GROUPS OF CLIENT FAMILIES

Level of Family Functioning

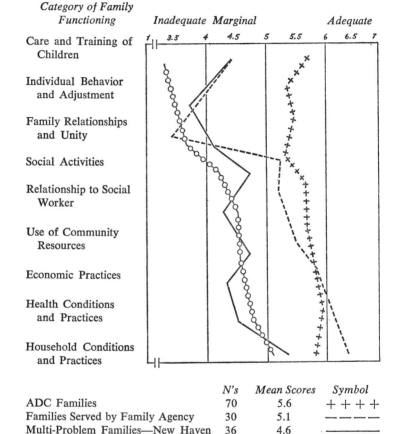

	N's	Mean Scores	Symbol
ADC Families	70	5.6	+ + + +
Families Served by Family Agency	30	5.1	— — — —
Multi-Problem Families—New Haven	36	4.6	————
Multi-Problem Families—St. Paul	150	4.5	0 0 0 0

Family Functioning is an instrument which is able to measure properties of behavior that are used diagnostically in
social work. Furthermore, it differentiates among client
groups which on an a priori basis are seen to differ from one
another. With this evidence on the validity of the scale let

TABLE 1. MEAN SCORES OF SOCIAL FUNCTIONING AND STANDARD DEVIATIONS FOR FOUR
CLIENT POPULATIONS

SERVICE SETTINGS

Category of Family Functioning	ADC Service (N=70)		Family Service (N=30)		Service to M-P Families New Haven (N=36)		Service to M-P Families St. Paul (N=150)	
	Means	*S.D.'s*	*Means*	*S.D.'s*	*Means*	*S.D.'s*	*Means*	*S.D.'s*
Care and Training of Children	5.7	.95	4.4	.83	4.4	.96	3.7	1.04
Individual Behavior and Adjustment	5.3	1.04	3.9	.71	3.9	.94	3.8	.81
Family Relationships and Unity	5.4	1.02	3.6	1.02	4.2	1.02	3.9	.93
Social Activities	5.3	.99	5.3	.97	4.9	.77	4.6	.79
Relationship to Social Worker	5.7	1.08	5.3	1.05	4.6	.81	4.7	.84
Use of Community Resources	5.7	.95	5.5	.80	4.9	.81	4.7	.86
Economic Practices	5.8	.77	5.8	.80	4.5	.89	4.8	.88
Health Conditions and Practices	5.9	.99	6.1	.83	4.6	1.01	4.9	1.06
Household Conditions and Practices	5.8	1.23	6.4	.87	5.3	1.45	5.1	1.42
Mean of Column Means	5.6	1.00	5.1	.88	4.6	.96	4.5	.96
S.D.'s of Mean of Means	.22	.12	.90	.11	.39	.19	.48	.19

us now apply it to an analysis of the functioning of a group of seriously disorganized families and compare their functioning pattern with that of families showing greater stability and adequacy in role relationships. The demonstration of differences in present family functioning, which will be statistically documented, is not seen as an end in itself but as a means of launching research into factors in the early life cycle of families associated with later family stability or disorganization. This effort at early identification of multi-problem families is seen as a beginning attempt to develop tools with which social work may examine its performance in the area of prevention.

NOTES FOR CHAPTER 3

[1] L. L. Geismar, *Report on Checklist Survey* (St. Paul, Minn.: Family Centered Project, 1957, mimeographed).

[2] Beverly Ayres and Joseph Lagey, *A Checklist Survey of Multi-Problem Families in Vancouver City* (Vancouver, B.C.: Community Chest and Councils of the Greater Vancouver Area, 1961, mimeographed).

[3] Bradley Buell and Associates, *Community Planning for Human Service* (New York: Columbia University Press, 1952), pp. 11-17.

[4] See Community Research Associates, *Matters of Fact for the National Conference on Appraising Family Needs* (New York: Community Research Associates, 1949).

[5] The St. Paul 1948 survey included 16 recreation and group work agencies; the Vancouver checklist survey covered 4; and the St. Paul 1957 checklist survey, none.

[6] Community Research Associates, *op. cit.*, pp. 50-53.

[7] For details, see *Ibid.*, Geismar, *op. cit.*, and Ayres and Lagey, *op. cit.*

[8] Community Service Society, *Searchlight on New York: A Progress Report on Human Welfare in New York City* (New York: Community Service Society, 1960), p. 37.

[9] Interestingly enough, another survey of a low-income housing project in Syracuse, New York, showed that approximately 8 per cent (54 out of 678) of the families were identified as problem families. See Charles V. Willie, Morton O. Wagenfeld, and Lee J. Cart, *The Effect of Social Service upon Rental Paying Patterns in Low Income Problem Families* (Syracuse, N.Y.: Youth Development Center, Syracuse University, 1962, mimeographed), p. 1.

[10] Ayres and Lagey, *op. cit.*, p. 34-40.

[11] L. L. Geismar and Beverly Ayres, *Families in Trouble* (St. Paul, Minn.: Family Centered Project of St. Paul, 1958), p. 48 ff.

[12] Bradley Buell and Associates, *op. cit.*, p. 9.

[13] Geismar and Ayres, *Families in Trouble, op. cit.*, p. 48 ff.

14 Social service exchanges were established by the early charity organizations as a means of systematizing relief giving in the community and to avoid duplication in providing money and services. With the concentration of relief-giving functions in the hands of large public agencies the exchange came to be viewed as a repository of information useful in the co-ordination of different services. Information at the exchange is generally limited to family's name, agency giving the service, data of case opening and closing. Some exchanges, like the St. Paul Central Registration Bureau, use a system of cross-indexing to yield information service to close relatives. In recent years in the wake of an increasing diversification of services and a trend toward selective registrations, many communities have closed down their exchanges.

15 Beverly Ayres, *Analysis of Central Registration Bureau Data on One Hundred Family Centered Project Families* (St. Paul, Minn.: Family Centered Project, May, 1957, mimeographed).

16 *Ibid.*, p. 5.

17 Michael La Sorte, "Differentiating Factors Between Multi-Problem and Non-Problem Families Registering with the Social Service Exchange in New Haven, Connecticut." Unpublished manuscript.

18 Beverly Ayres, *op. cit.*, p. 17.

19 *Ibid.*

20 La Sorte, *op. cit.*

21 Geismar and Ayres, *Families in Trouble, op. cit.*, pp. 74-75.

22 Ayres, *op. cit.*, pp. 5-19.

23 *Ibid.*

24 L. L. Geismar and Beverly Ayres, *Measuring Family Functioning. A Manual on a Method for Evaluating the Social Functioning of Disorganized Families* (St. Paul, Minn.: Family Centered Project, 1960).

25 L. L. Geismar and Beverly Ayres, in association with K. Tinker, *Patterns of Change in Problem Families* (St. Paul, Minn.: Family Centered Project, 1959).

L. L. Geismar and Beverly Ayres, "A Method for Evaluating the Social Functioning of Families Under Treatment," *Social Work*, Vol. 4, No. 1, Jan., 1959, pp. 102-108.

L. L. Geismar, "The Multi-Problem Family: Significance of Research Findings," *The Social Welfare Forum*, 1960 (New York: Columbia University Press, 1960), pp. 166-179.

Ludwig L. Geismar, "The Social Functioning of the ADC Family," *The Welfare Reporter*, Vol. XIV, Number 3, July, 1963, pp. 43-54.

26 For details see Geismar and Ayres, *Measuring Family Functioning, op. cit.*

27 *Ibid.*, pp. 7-20.

28 The three levels spelled out here are: the midpoint—marginal functioning; the left anchor point—inadequate; the right anchor point—adequate functioning. Additional scale points not defined in the levels of Social Functioning scheme but designed to provide for finer gradations of judgment between the anchor points were called: near inadequate; below marginal; above marginal; near adequate functioning. The method of evaluation was thus based upon a seven-point continuum which was applied to nine areas and 26 sub-areas of family functioning.

[29] Geismar and Ayres, *Measuring Family Functioning, op. cit.*

[30] For details of the method and tests of reliability to which the rating technique had been subjected, see *Ibid.,* pp. 2-173.

[31] *Ibid.,* pp. 21-42.

[32] Scale analysis showed that the data came close to satisfying but did not fully satisfy all the criteria for determining scalability. For a more detailed discussion of this subject, see L. L. Geismar, Michael A. La Sorte, and Beverly Ayres, "Measuring Family Disorganization," *Marriage and Family Living,* Vol. XXIV, No. 1, Feb., 1962, pp. 52-60.

[33] See pertinent articles in Samuel A. Stouffer, Louis Guttman, *et al., Measurement and Prediction* (Princeton, N.J., Princeton University Press, 1950).

See, also, Matilda W. Riley, John W. Riley, Jr., and Jackson Toby, *Sociological Studies in Scale Analysis* (New Brunswick, N.J., Rutgers University Press, 1954).

[34] See especially *Reaching the Unreached,* Youth Board Monograph No. 5 (New York: New York City Youth Board, 1958).

Geismar and Ayres, *Families in Trouble, op. cit.*

Janet E. Weinandy, *Families Under Stress* (Syracuse, N.Y.: Youth Development Center, Syracuse University, 1962).

Leontine R. Young, *Study of the Behavior Syndromes of Parents of Neglected and Abused Children* (New York: Columbia University, unpublished doctoral thesis, 1962).

[35] Geismar and Ayres, *Families in Trouble, op. cit.,* and *Patterns of Change in Problem Families, op. cit.*

[36] Geismar and Ayres, *op. cit.*

[37] L. L. Geismar, *Applying an Operational Definition of Family Functioning in Determining Need for Services.* Paper read at the Annual Meeting of the American Sociological Society (Washington, D.C., Aug., 1962, mimeographed).

[38] Claire Selltiz, Marie Jahoda, *et al., Research Methods in Social Relations* (New York: Holt, Rinehart, and Winston, Inc., 1961), p. 155.

[39] L. L. Geismar, *Family Diagnosis—Similarity and Variance in Different Settings* (Rutgers, N.J.: Graduate School of Social Work, Rutgers —The State University, 1962, unpublished paper, mimeographed).

[40] This figure indicates that roughly 8 per cent of the families in this low-income housing development are seriously disorganized. This is almost four times the rate found for two metropolitan areas, St. Paul, Minn., and Vancouver, B.C. These areas are more heterogeneous in social status than the New Haven project area.

[41] With reference to the statistical significance of findings the question can be asked whether the differences among the mean scores of family functioning are greater than might be expected by chance. An answer is possible if we accept the assumption, at least partially defensible, that the client groups selected in this study are representative of larger universes of client families served in the respective agencies. The median test of the significance of difference yields a chi square value of 65.70 (1 d.f. $p < .001$) which permits a rejection of the hypothesis that differences in functioning are due to chance.

[42] E. Garinczi, N. Larson, L. Miller, P. Rekstad, N. H. Ian, *A Study*

of Multi-Problem Families from the St. Paul Family Centered Project: Factors Distinguishing Multi-Problem Families for Whom a Court Petition of Neglect Was Filed from Those for Whom It Was Not Filed (Minneapolis, Minn: School of Social Work, University of Minnesota, June, 1961, M.S.W. thesis, unpublished).

[43] Chi squares for a 2 x 2 table were 6.38 (p. < .01) at the beginning of treatment and 34.81 (p < .001) at the time of closing.

[44] Walda Ciafone, Florence M. Bernstein, *et al., Relationship of Family Functioning to Anomie, Social Class, and Other Related Factors* (New Brunswick, N.J., Graduate School of Social Work, Rutgers:—The State University, June, 1963, unpublished M.S.W. Thesis), p. 20.

CHAPTER 4:

STABLE AND DISORGANIZED
FAMILIES

A STUDY OF SEVENTY-FIVE
LOW-INCOME FAMILIES[1]

The research described in this chapter represents an attempt
to pinpoint the basic characteristics of the multi-problem
family. It is an effort in the direction of formulating hypotheses, to be tested in longitudinal studies, on the processes leading to family disorganization. Early identification
of the phenomenon of family disorganization is seen as a
primary goal in the total research effort. Such identification
represents a cherished objective in social welfare because it
holds the key to prevention of family disorganization.

Family disorganization and its consequences for the community as well as the individual family has been of concern

to many family and social welfare researchers. Varying approaches and different instruments have been employed by these researchers to study aspects of family disorganization. The research, in general, has aimed at defining the concept of family disorganization, identifying it in the community, and determining what factors in the family history are relevant to a better understanding of their present state of disorganization. This latter concern represents part of an impetus during periods following nation-wide crises such as the Depression, World War II, and the postwar recessions. Recent studies linking economic dependency, crime, and juvenile delinquency to family disorganization have spurred research efforts directed toward discovering antecedents of the problem.

Viewing family disorganization as a consequence has taken at least two forms: (1) large-scale official statistics, and (2) crisis situations experienced by the family. Mowrer[2] used divorce and desertion as indices of family disorganization and related these to such variables as density of population and other ecological characteristics to note differential rates. Bernard[3] studied remarriages and correlated antecedent factors by collecting data on socio-economic status, age of parents, attitudes, duration of first marriage, and so on.

What might be termed temporary family disorganization centered about specific circumstances and time periods was studied by Hill, Cavan and Ranck, and Komarovsky. Hill[4] studied stresses experienced by the family with the departure and return of the war veteran; and Cavan and Ranck[5] and Komarovsky[6] did research on the impact of the Depression and unemployment on family relationships. These studies have paid particular attention to events and situations outside the family system noting the resulting effects upon the functioning patterns of family members.[7] Attention has also been given by Goode to the problem of intrafamilial conflict resulting mainly from family interaction, and by Le Masters to the mechanisms brought into play to deal with these conflicts.[8]

THE STUDY SETTING

The families who were to be studied live in the Farnam Courts housing project, which is part of a much larger neighborhood in the central area of New Haven, Connecticut. The project, established in January, 1942, comprises three hundred apartments. Approximately 40 per cent of the population is Negro and 10 per cent is Puerto Rican. About one-third of the remaining families are of Italian descent, and the remainder represent a variety of nationalities. In 1960 the median number of persons per household was 3.8. This relatively low figure may be accounted for by the fact that thirty elderly couples and fifteen individuals over sixty-five live in one-bedroom apartments in the housing project. The average move-out rate since the inception of the project has been 15.2 per cent per year. With the elimination of surrounding houses and commercial structures as part of a city-wide urban renewal program, the project has been moving increasingly toward physical isolation as a residential area.

In common with most cities in the United States, New Haven has experienced a slight decrease in population in its central area during the past twenty years. Correlated with this trend there has been an increasing deterioration of the central area with the emigration of old ethnic groups from the residential areas to suburbia or other cities and a movement of new migrants, mostly Negro and Puerto Rican, into the city. To get a better understanding of the environmental features of the neighborhood of which the housing project is a part, census data and other historical sources are used to describe its main characteristics.[9]

The neighborhood can be traced back to the early 1800's.

The city at that time had the core of its population about one-half mile away extending out in the opposite direction. The present main thoroughfares of the area were opened up to the traffic of the day about this time. Although sparsely settled, this area already had its unique features.

From 1810 to the 1860's the housing consisted of shanty-like dwellings, hurriedly constructed, with interspersed plots of cultivated land and roving farm animals. Two somewhat distinct Negro groups lived on the fringes and within the neighborhood itself. Along the main street and just south lay an area of itinerant laborers, poverty stricken Negroes, and others of the working class of that day. The saloons of the area—with their cheap liquor, prostitution, and frequent brawls—were the center of the community's social life and attracted many townsfolk seeking entertainment. Along the street skirting the area, or what was known then as Negro Lane, were the residences of the more prosperous Negroes of the day.

The beginning of the large European immigration circa 1830, consisting mostly of Irish laborers on patronage, brought a change to the area. The low-rent values of the neighborhood and closeness of the factories that produced carriages, hardware, leather goods, and, later, rubber material and guns, attracted the immigrants in ever-increasing numbers. The Negroes, scattered throughout the city during this period, gradually concentrated themselves on the other side of the city until by 1890 more than half of the Negro population was so situated, but the original neighborhood consisted mostly of Irish, Italian, Polish, and Russian immigrants with their families.

The influx of European immigrants into the state got under way in the 1860's with the start of mass immigration and reached its climax during the 1900's. Those foreign-born groups distributed themselves throughout the state with the city receiving the largest percentage of Italians and Irish.

The immigrants helped to increase the population of the city substantially from 1860 to 1920. They settled in fairly well-defined areas of the city, with our neighborhood predominantly populated by first- and second-generation immigrants, especially Italians, up to 1940. From about 1880 to the end of World War II this district has been part of, what Gans calls, an "Urban Village" of Italian immigrants.[10] The neighborhood at any one time had only a sprinkling of English-Welsh foreign stock. After 1940, the composition of the neighborhood's population took on a changing aspect. The population as a whole has decreased steadily, and the number of Negroes in the area has increased tenfold. Beginning in the late 1940's, there was a large influx of Negroes from the Southern states. By 1960, Negroes comprised 23 per cent of the neighborhood population.

One area, The Square, was in the early 1800's a fashionable, residential suburban section, but by the turn of the century its land values decreased with the spilling over of immigrant workers and factories from the surrounding area. The past affluence of The Square can still be seen in the architectural design of some of the older houses.

The first statistical analysis of the neighborhood, carried out in the 1930's, revealed a mainly residential area with manufacturing and wholesale and retail outlets along the main streets and fringes of the district. Residential meant a preponderance of flats containing families of relatively low socio-economic standing, and with the following social indices higher than the city average: birth rate, juvenile delinquency, incidence of tuberculosis, and unemployment. Basically, these area characteristics, plus a few others, seem to have changed little since that time.

A comparison of the predominant type of dwelling structures in the city and in the neighborhood since 1940 reveals that the proportion of one-family houses in the neighborhood has decreased somewhat. The general mode of housing is a building containing three to five family units. Rent per unit is much less than the city's median rent. Over the past thirty years, however, the median rent level in the neighborhood has shown an increase beyond that for the city as a whole and is approaching the city's level. This rise cannot be attributed to recent construction of dwelling units in the neighborhood. The only units built in the area since 1940 are those in the housing project; the majority of other houses were built before 1919. Between 1940 and 1950, however, the number of five-family houses increased by more than two hundred, an indication of the possible subdivision of larger apartments into smaller ones.

The condition of the dwelling units themselves has deteriorated steadily since 1940. In 1960, one-quarter of the units was rated by the Census Bureau as dilapidated or deteriorating. The total for the city as a whole was slightly below that of the neighborhood, but in both cases almost one-half of the dwelling units occupied by Negroes had deteriorated.

The vast majority of families in the neighborhood, both white and Negro, are renters rather than owners of their dwelling units. This situation is much the same as it has been for the past three or four decades, and possibly since the beginning of settlement in the 1800's. The comparatively small number of home owners are chiefly white, although there has been some increase in the number of units owned by Negroes in recent years.

The average family size has been decreasing steadily during the past thirty years and is now about three persons per household. The trend is the same for the city, but the shrinkage in family size has not been so great. The population density per residential acreage in the area has also declined, concurrent with declining family size. Although the density remains far above that of the city, it has decreased steadily and is, as of 1960, 50 per cent lower than in 1920.

A large part of this decrease can be attributed to the razing of dilapidated units in the 1950's in conjunction with a city-wide redevelopment program. The number of households containing nonrelatives or boarders has also decreased since 1950.

Despite these trends, crowded conditions in the homes of the neighborhood were much in evidence in 1960. Nineteen per cent of the housing units had more than one person per room as compared with 9 per cent for the city. The Negro families had less space per person than the white families, with a ratio of more than one person per room in almost four out of ten dwelling units.

The neighborhood's residents move less than do the families of the city as a whole, either within the city limits or beyond them. A review of the families moving into the housing project revealed that those who were already residents of the city came predominantly from the immediate neighborhood or from one quite similar in socio-economic status.

In the present century, the occupational stratum most strongly represented in the area appears to be similar to the original inhabitants' socio-economic status. White collar workers—the professional, technical, and clerical types—are much underrepresented. Most occupations fall into the semiskilled variety with a slight overrepresentation of service and unskilled workers. The income level, below the city's median, reflects this low socio-economic status of the neighborhood residents.

The unemployment rate is not only higher than the city's rate but also appears to be on the upgrade, despite relatively prosperous times. Relief of all types, especially financial, is more pronounced in the neighborhood than in areas that are quite similar in socio-economic status.

During the past thirty years the population age pyramid has shown a movement toward a younger population for the city, with an accentuation of this trend in the neighborhood. The population composition has changed from approximately the same proportion of young children to adults approaching middle age, with few persons over 65, to a sizable increase in pre-teen and early teen-age children, a sharp decrease in middle-age adults, and a larger proportion of persons over 65. The neighborhood, therefore, has more children and young adults under twenty-one than does the city as a whole.

SELECTING THE SAMPLE

In the present study, seventy-five selected families in a public housing project were classified by the use of the Profile of Family Functioning into three subsamples differing clearly in their positions on the stability-disorganization continuum. Cross tabulations were then made between the three subgroups and selected premarital and postmarital variables in family structure and functioning.

In selecting the sample for the study from families living in a housing project, the disadvantage of possible lack of representativeness of the population appears to be outweighed by certain definite advantages. It was possible to control such factors as residence and to a large extent income, since a family in order to qualify for project housing cannot have means which would enable it to rent or buy an adequate private home. Moreover, the housing project already had an active research project, the Neighborhood Improvement Project, whose work had prepared the ground for ready access to the families living in the development.

The initial criteria were: (1) one- or two-parent families with one or more children under 18 in the home, and (2) families with at least one year's residence in the housing project.

Since one of the goals of the study was to compare disorganized with stable families, the usual random sampling technique was not used to obtain the sample. Instead, every effort was made to select from among the three hundred families in the project those which, in addition to meeting the initial criteria above, distributed themselves at the two ends of the stability-disorganization continuum. The most malfunctioning among the project residents had already been located by reading local agency records and by home interviews in order to extend to them intensive casework service. The remainder of the project families were reviewed to select the most stable, also on the basis of agency records and information from the housing authority staff.

This procedure resulted in the selection of 36 disorganized families (already in treatment) and 43 stable families. As explained below, the number in the latter group was later reduced to 39. The total number of families studied was 75. The two methods of selection, identification on the basis of professional judgment and measurement by applying the scale, correlated $+.89$ (Gamma coefficient). This coefficient does not represent a complete one-to-one relationship (see Table 2). Looking at only the High and Low distributions in the table showing cross tabulation of the two methods, it is evident that the a priori method was quite successful in predicting the results of measurement based on interviews. Only five of the 53 High-Low families are in the minor diagonal. The chief advantage of measurement is in discriminating in a more highly refined manner degree of functioning. The Median distribution points this out with a tendency to place most of its families in the Problem cell but with 9 of the 22 Medians scored a priori as Stable. The Medians, then, those families somewhat on the margin between disorganization and organization, are separated out by the measurement method achieving greater homogeneity in the extreme groups rather than having the Median families placed partly in both Stable and Problem subsamples as the Judgment method would have it.

TABLE 2. COMPARISON OF PROFESSIONAL JUDGMENT (A PRIORI) AND MEASUREMENT BASED ON INTERVIEWS (A POSTERIORI) IN DETERMINING LEVEL OF FAMILY FUNCTIONING

Interview and Measurement Method	Judgment Method		
	Stable	Problem	Totals
High	26	1	27
Median	9	13	22
Low	4	22	26
Totals	39	36	75
	gamma = +.89		

OBTAINING THE DATA[11]

Data on the families in both groups were collected by means of interviews. The disorganized families, already in treatment, were, with a few exceptions, interviewed by their own caseworkers. Thus, the problem of accessibility was relevant only for the stable families.

The interviewers, when approaching the stable families, presented their aims as follows:

• "I am working for the Neighborhood Improvement Project (NIP) serving this area." If the respondent was unfamiliar with the organization, the interviewer gave a brief explanation of what it was.

• "Your family is recognized as getting along quite well, and as having been able to handle successfully such problems as have occurred in the past."

• "We are asking for your co-operation in a study in order that NIP can learn more about the problems you and others in your family have run into and the ways in which you dealt with these problems. This information could help us teach others how to cope with problems in life." If the respondent at that point asked for examples of the kind of questions the interviewer would ask, some sample questions were presented.

Initially we had hoped to experiment with different approaches to the families—telephone calls or letters preceding the visit and unannounced visits. The interviewers, who were experienced social workers, used the three approach techniques; but, as it turned out, only four of the 43 families scheduled to be interviewed refused to participate in the study. Thus no analysis of differential success based on the different approaches could be made. All three served equally well to gain access to the family.

The reasons underlying the four rejections did not appear to represent interviewer failures. Case one was visited by two interviewers, a male interviewer and then a female interviewer after a seven-months' interval. Both interviewers made nearly identical comments indicating that the woman was emotionally upset, shed tears, and found it too painful to talk about facts related to her former husband and circumstances leading to her divorce. Case two was adamant about not wanting to be bothered and could not be located at a second try. In case three, in which there were problems of eviction and placement of the children, the woman expressed over the telephone her dislike of social workers and used abusive language. Nevertheless, when the interviewer called she admitted him to the home. As the interviewer moved into the personal area, he encountered extreme resistance and gave up after 45 minutes. In case four, the husband, seemingly intoxicated, confronted the interviewer in a very belligerent manner and drove him out of the home. The "safety first principle" won out over scientific considerations and precluded a return visit to this family.

The fact that the interviewers represented an organization known to many respondents may have contributed to the low rejection rate. It should be noted that no negative sanctions, stated or implicit, accompanied the request for participation in the study, and no positive sanctions, such as payment for time lost or an offer of services, were used in the approach to the family.

All the interviewers were given training to acquaint them with the interview schedule and the goals of the research. This training involved two or three sessions conducted by the research staff before the schedule was pretested. After the pretest the schedules were analyzed to determine whether the areas of behavior under exploration received meaningful answers in terms of both the interviewers' grasp of the queries and the respondents' ability to understand the manner in which the questions were posed. On the basis of this pretest the schedule underwent minor revisions and was then used for interviewing the 75 families.

The average length of the interviews ranged from two to three hours, in one or two and sometimes more sessions with the families. Because of the nature of the data, it was necessary for the interviewer at least to "see" all family members and not just the respondent for the family. Hence return trips were sometimes necessary, but the multiple visits were on the whole accepted by the families with few negative reactions.

Reliability of Response

A cross-check system was used to determine the correctness of the demographic information. The interviewer obtained data from the client which was already available to us through the records of the Housing Authority but not available to the interviewers. Such information included marriage dates, education of parents, number and ages of children, and the like. The contradictions between the data in the record and those obtained in the interview were too few to justify statistical analysis. Contradictions which did exist on sensitive subjects, such as the time of childbirths in relation to marriage dates, led us to conclude that the social work interviewers rather than the Housing Authority were given the correct information about situations in which accepted standards of behavior had been compromised. The remarkable fact about this conclusion is not that the correct information was withheld from the authorities but rather that it was supplied voluntarily to the interviewers.

In one instance, as a result of administrative error, a complete interview with one of the families in treatment was repeated after a six-month interval with strikingly similar results. The woman who was inadvertently subjected to two interviews had been under casework treatment off and on. It is possible that such readiness to supply information may be the function of a phenomenon more common in the lower than the higher socio-economic classes. We would call it, for lack of a better term, reaction of the "professional interviewee." As a result of a long conditioning process, the professional interviewee is ready to answer all questions raised and is likely to have many pat answers at the presentation of the stimulus.

Success in Response Frequency

The families' level of social functioning, reflecting differential degrees of stability in family relationships and of reciprocity in the performance of family roles, was thought to have some effect upon the way the heads of families, usually the mothers, responded to the interview. The patterns of behavior in the performance of socially expected tasks necessary for maintaining the family were seen as reflected in the way a family was able to respond to the request for an interview and to communicate information. Social work research has provided beginning evidence that there is a direct association between the latter factor and a family's ability to relate to a treatment person.[12] It was assumed that such a relationship would hold true also with regard to the research interviewer.

The 39 stable families who were not in treatment were divided into three groups called "High," "Median," and "Low," according to their levels of social functioning as measured by the St. Paul scale. Each interviewer made a notation on whether he was received by a family in a guarded manner with initial suspicion or without any apparent mistrust. The responses of 17 families fit the former pattern, those of 22 families fit the latter. When the three groups (which happened to consist of 13 families each) were cross-tabulated by initial response to the interviewer, a correlation (Gamma) of +.50 was found. That is to say, suspicious response tended to be associated with a lower level of social functioning.

Level of social functioning also was related to failure to answer questions, at least in the 39 nontreatment families. The Low functioning families were found to answer 1.6 questions less, on the average, than those in the High group. For the 36 disorganized families (who were in treatment) no major differences were found in this respect. It is very probable that treatment, focusing heavily on communication and the establishment of relationships, had the effect of neutralizing differences in response failure between poorly and well-functioning groups.

What types of questions among those posed were most likely to meet with no response? An answer to this was sought by analyzing response patterns of all the 75 families studied. By and large, the more abstract and conceptually more difficult queries, such as respondents' expectations of marriage, encountered most response failures, ranging between 12 and 23 per cent. On questions pertaining to sex, response failures were low except on the item which sought to establish where the respondent first learned about the subject. Twenty-eight per cent failed to answer this question. The families found it relatively easy to talk about such personal matters as positive and negative incentives to getting married, and problems and conflicts during the engagement period and after marriage. The completed schedules on the whole are a testimony to the interviewees' readiness to make their lives, even in their intimate aspects, available to the inquirer.

Limitations of the Research Method

One area of the schedule failed to bring out data that could be used for analysis. Information relating to various factors in the more extended life cycle, such as frequency and types of crisis situations, and reactions of family members to crises, showed no relationship to present family malfunctioning. In analyzing these data the weakness of the ex post facto method based on recall, in contrast to the longitudinal design in which the families would be followed through time, seemed most evident. Occurrences in the past not anchored in time to landmarks in life, such as school leaving, marriage, and birth of first child, may be forgotten, repressed, poorly remembered, or highly colored by later experiences. The timing and spacing of the crisis situations, seemingly of some theoretical importance,[13] could not be studied with great accuracy in the present design.

The ex post facto design, sometimes referred to as a study-in-reverse, proceeds from the phenomenon to be explained to a gathering, in an historical fashion, of data which might have impinged upon the phenomenon. This consequent to antecedent form of research has many pitfalls relative to reliability and validity.[14] A sounder procedure for more substantive data would be to design a longitudinal study of family disorganization. With the limited time and inadequate knowledge of the relevant variables this procedure did not appear feasible. It is for this reason in particular that the present study should be viewed as exploratory in nature.

Despite its drawbacks, the ex post facto design remains a sound approximation to a longitudinal study and can give suggestive data and sound insights in areas of behavior associated with family malfunctioning. With these limitations in mind the findings presented on correlates of family disorganization remain tentative until more rigid procedures for testing hypotheses are designed and carried out.

PROCEDURE OF ANALYSIS

Research on the 75 families which comprised the sample population had two aspects: (1) an analysis of the patterns of present family functioning, and (2) an analysis of background factors and their association with present functioning patterns.

In exploring the first aspect, the first step was to establish the location of each family on the scale of general criteria of total family functioning.[15] This anchored the families on the degree to which their behavior is consistent with, or deviates from, general community approved, normative family behavior. After each family was judged on each of the family functioning categories, it was assigned an over-all family functioning score. This procedure appeared to be justified on the basis of the scalability of the measuring instrument, the Profile of Family Functioning.[16] The 75 families, identified in this manner according to their present functioning patterns, were divided into three groups: Low, Median, and High, numbering 26, 22, and 27 families, respectively.

In respect to the second aspect of the research, it should be noted that most studies of antecedent factors in family disorganization have had as one of their primary goals the identification of those families, early in their life cycle, who tend to become disorganized at a later date. Such studies have been fruitful in many ways in isolating indicators of malfunctioning and/or eventual dissolution of the family. A major weakness, however, is the establishment of indicators of the phenomenon when the concept to be evaluated remains unstandardized or subject to great variations.[17] Divorce rate as a reflection of family disorganization is an example of an indicator that is limited in scope, with few of its properties systematically assessed, and its prevalence readily subject to legal and administrative variations over time and space.

The methodology employed in the present study in the search for background correlates in disorganized families follows many of the basic procedures used in previous studies. The main difference in our present approach is the more precise manner of conceptualizing and grouping cases whose early functioning is to be explored.

Before proceeding to the next sections which present patterns of family functioning and profiles of two families, it is pertinent to note two basic items: control factors in the collection of the data and the structural characteristics of the families studied.

Control Factors

Even though a purposive sample selection technique was used in obtaining the population for the study, it appeared desirable also to control for at least two factors: the family member to be interviewed and the family ethnic affiliation. The woman in the family was taken as the family member most likely to furnish data on her family. She was the one who would be most accessible to an interview, probably most co-operative, and in terms of the research design the one most likely to have knowledge of the kinds of information desired. By keeping the interviewee a constant factor, greater reliability in response among the families would be assured.

Three main ethnic groupings are represented in the 300 families in the housing project: White, Negro, and Puerto Rican. By keeping in mind the ethnic distribution, possible unique functioning patterns within the ethnic groups would not enter as a biasing factor. At least between the High and Low groups ethnicity was fairly well taken into account on an aggregate basis. The Puerto Ricans, representing about 5 to 10 per cent of the housing project, contributed only two families to the sample population. Table 3 gives relevant data on these control factors by functioning level.

Structural Characteristics

The structural aspects of the families showed some similarity and some variance. The similarity in structure is most noticeable in that almost all families were nuclear in type. Only two families had an individual in the household who was not of the biological family unit; this situation could be expected, considering housing authority policy. The other structural aspects have greater variance (Table 3).

The most apparent variances between functioning levels is in the family life cycle stage and parental age. The Low group contains much younger families with approximately the same number of sons and daughters, but the children are much younger—mostly under ten years of age. The Low families still retain the great majority of all their biological offspring as dependents and tend to have larger families. Parental age, except for the Median group of men, varies directly with level of functioning. Well beyond one-half of the Low group parents are under forty years of age.

The range of family income quite surprisingly starts from a low of around $1560 and reaches a high of almost $9500 a year. But half of the families in the Low group have incomes of less than $2800 a year, and half of the families in the Median and High groups have incomes of over $3000 a year. The smaller total incomes in the Low group can be accounted for partly by the fact that a greater proportion are supported through public funds, such as Aid to Dependent Children and General Assistance. The other factor is the number of persons in the household who contribute to the total yearly income. The breadwinner for the Low group is predominantly the husband when he is in the household. This is true also in the High group but a larger proportion of the income can be attributed to varying amounts of money brought in by the children and wives.

The marital status of the 75 families differs little. Divorce

TABLE 3. CONTROL AND FAMILY STRUCTURAL VARIABLES
BY LEVEL OF FUNCTIONING (IN PERCENTAGES)

	High	Median	Low
Control Factors:			
Wife Interviewed	93	100	96
Negro Families	44	32	46
Structural Variables:			
Both parents in household	59	50	46
Couples permanently separated	33	41	42
Household unit: nuclear family	96	100	96
Marriage date 18 years ago or less	44	59	73
Family Life Cycle Stage: Young Adult families or with some children launched	41	23	12
Ratio of boys to girls in families	48	56	55
Male children aged 10 or over	67	53	40
Female children aged 10 or over	70	59	37
Families with 3 or more children	59	73	69
Present age: Men under 40	25	17	59
Women under 40	38	53	64
Annual family income over $3000 (1961)	52	42	39
Family income derived wholly or in part from public funds	39	47	70

is the main reason why the husband is absent from the home, followed by death, separation (legal and nonlegal), and desertion, in descending order of frequency.

PATTERNS OF PRESENT FAMILY FUNCTIONING

Table 4 shows the main category and total scores of family functioning for the 75 families by High, Median, and Low Functioning groups. For each category an index of social disorganization had been computed. This index represents an effort to assess systematically the difference in social functioning between the High and Low groups, relative to the degree of malfunctioning of the Low group. The index of social disorganization was arrived at by dividing the category mean score for the Low group into the difference

TABLE 4. MAIN CATEGORY MEAN SCORES FOR HIGH, MEDIAN, AND LOW FUNCTIONING GROUPS

Main Categories	High	Median	Low	Disorganization Index
Individual Behavior and Adjustment	6.33	4.73	3.65	.734
Family Relationships and Unity	6.33	4.68	3.73	.697
Care and Training of Children	6.59	4.95	3.92	.681
Health Conditions and Practices	6.41	5.50	4.26	.504
Use of Community Resources	6.48	5.41	4.46	.452
Social Activities	6.48	5.18	4.46	.452
Economic Practices	6.22	5.05	4.31	.443
Home Conditions and Household Practices	6.88	6.18	4.85	.418
Mean of Categories	6.47	5.21	4.21	
S.D. of Means	.19	.46	.38	
Number of Families	27	22	26	

between the High and the Low groups. By this method we note that the index is a function of both difference between High group and Low group scores and size of functioning score of the most problematic group. The high index number denotes greater malfunctioning of the Low group, relative to the adequately functioning families.

The eight main categories in Table 4 are listed in order of size of the disorganization index. (One category, *Relationship to Social Worker*, is omitted from this analysis since it is not applicable to the stable families.) Areas showing the greatest power of discrimination are in the category *Individual Behavior and Adjustment*, representing role clusters or the total of roles played by each family member, and in the category *Family Relationships and Unity*. The two instrumental categories, *Economic Practices* and *Home Conditions and Household Practices*, differentiate less sharply between the well-functioning and the malfunctioning families. Other studies of problem families have revealed a characteristic pattern of social malfunctioning, chiefly in the area of intrafamilial relationships.[18]

When we look at the High, Median, and Low groups it is clearly evident that they are differentiated by level of functioning. None of the eight categories overlaps between groups; and each category mean decreases in a linear fashion from High to Median to Low, revealing three quite independent levels of functioning. The Highs' functioning pattern varies very little (S.D. of Mean of Categories is .19) and is characterized by an almost straight profile line (see Figure 3). All categories are functioning well into the adequate side of the scale and they differ from one another by not more than .66 of a scale step. This largest difference is noted between the categories of *Economic Practices* and *Home Conditions and Household Practices*. Apparently, as a group, the High families are quite homogeneous in the manner in which they carry out family tasks. This homogeneity may, in part, result from the arbitrarily designed limits of the family functioning scale at point seven. If the scale had been constructed to handle the more refined estimations of adequate family behavior, then possibly larger differences would have appeared. Nevertheless, relatively greater homogeneity of the High group would have been apparent. All regions of family life are represented by behavior conforming more or less to community expectations and relatively free of stress and conflict which threaten the welfare of family members.

In the Median subsample the distribution of scores about the category means shows more scatter (S.D. .46) and less homogeneity than is the case with the adequate families. A somewhat characteristic problem profile begins to take shape with the intrafamilial categories functioning closer to the

FIGURE 3. PROFILES OF FAMILY FUNCTIONING OF HIGH, MEDIAN, AND LOW FUNCTIONING GROUPS BY DISORGANIZATION INDEX

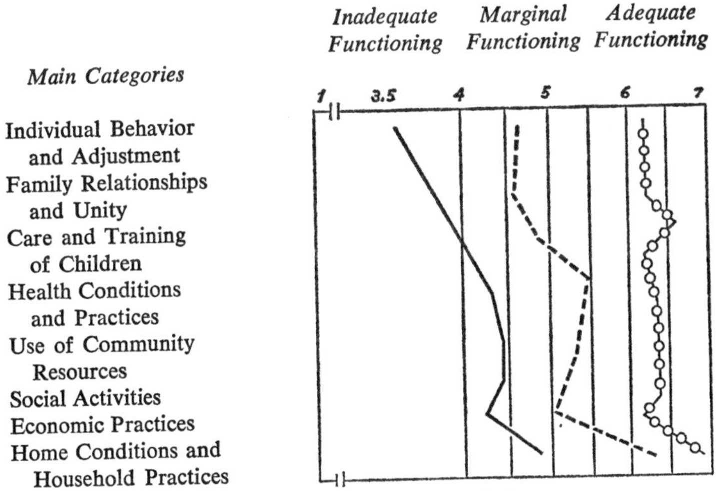

	N	Symbol
High	27	o o o o o o
Median	22	- - - - - - -
Low	26	————

marginal level and the extrafamilial and instrumental areas extending out toward the adequate side of the scale and only reaching it in *Home Conditions and Household Practices.* This subgroup functions in the above-marginal range of the scale, with a full-scale step-and-one-half separating the lowest from the highest category.

The Low group, representing the disorganized families, reveals 1.20 scale steps diversity (S.D. .38) between categories and a more sharply delineated profile. The intrafamilial categories are found well into the inadequate side of the scale with no mean score reaching the above-marginal level. Although the Low group is not so homogeneous in content as the High group, it does have less intrasample heterogeneity than the Median group.

In the analysis which follows, the High and Low groups are treated as "pure" samples indicative of nonproblem and problem family behavior, respectively. The Median group, on the other hand, is a "mixed" sample composed of families that as a group reveal greater variation in family functioning. The chief focal points are High and Low comparisons, with the Medians serving as an indicator of the direction of differences.

The three groups were determined, of course, by finding, with the aid of total functioning scores, the positions of the families on the total family functioning continuum and then arbitrarily splitting them up into the three subsamples. The clear separation of the subgroups by category and subcategory (see below) revealed the relationships of the categories to the criterion of selection—the total family functioning score of each group of families.

The eight categories of social functioning are subdivided into 24 subcategories. The main categories represent composites of their respective subcategories by definition, taking into account the theoretical relatedness of certain behavior dimensions. Thus *Social Activities* is seen as being composed of formal and informal social activities. *Care and Training of Children* is seen as a function of physical care and training methods. A descriptively more detailed analysis can be carried out with the Profile data by studying the subcategory scores relative to their magnitude and differences between High and Low groups.

TABLE 5. SUBCATEGORY MEAN SCORE BY FUNCTIONING LEVEL
(WITH H-L DIFFERENCE IN MEAN SCORE)

Subcategory	High	Median	Low	H-L Difference
1. Marital relationship	5.88	4.60	3.16	2.72
2. Parent-child relationships	6.19	4.50	3.76	2.43
3. Sibling relationships	6.52	4.95	4.50	2.02
4. Family solidarity	6.41	4.71	3.62	2.79
5. Father	5.75	4.43	3.07	2.68
6. Mother	6.30	4.64	3.56	2.74
7. Children 10 years and over	6.42	4.84	3.75	2.67
8. Children under 10	6.42	5.18	4.32	2.10
9. Physical care	6.88	6.00	4.42	2.46
10. Training methods and emotional care	6.33	4.25	3.54	2.79
11. Informal associations	6.37	5.14	4.72	1.65
12. Formal associations	6.22	5.15	4.42	1.80
13. Source and amount of income	5.77	5.10	4.36	1.41
14. Job situation	6.38	5.39	4.71	1.67
15. Use of money	6.48	5.45	4.22	2.26
16. Physical facilities	6.67	6.09	5.04	1.63
17. Housekeeping standards	6.96	6.18	4.73	2.23
18. Health problems	6.50	5.41	4.25	2.25
19. Health practices	6.62	5.67	4.22	2.40
20. School	6.30	5.20	4.52	1.78
21. Church	6.61	6.00	6.13	.48
22. Health resources	6.61	5.62	4.48	2.13
23. Social agencies	5.94	5.10	4.26	1.68
24. Recreational facilities	6.33	5.30	4.57	1.76

Table 5 lists the subcategory values of High, Median, and Low functioning families grouped by main categories. Differences between the High and Low groups are also given. Table 6 gives a rank order listing of subcategories by index of disorganization. As in the main categories, the largest differences between the problem and nonproblem groups are predominantly in the area of intrafamilial functioning and the individual behavior of family members. The subcategories with a low order of association to problem functioning are concerned mostly with instrumental activities and community interaction. The low index value of church

TABLE 6. RANK ORDER OF SUBCATEGORIES BY INDEX
OF DISORGANIZATION

Subcategory	Index
1. Father	.872
2. Marital relationship	.860
10. Training methods and emotional care	.788
4. Family solidarity	.770
6. Mother	.769
7. Children 10 years and over	.712
2. Parent-child relationships	.646
19. Health practices	.568
9. Physical care	.556
15. Use of money	.535
18. Health problems	.529
8. Children under 10	.486
22. Health resources	.475
17. Housekeeping standards	.471
3. Sibling relationships	.448
12. Formal associations	.407
23. Social agencies	.394
20. School	.393
24. Recreational agencies	.385
14. Job situation	.354
11. Informal associations	.349
16. Physical facilities	.323
13. Source and amount of income	.323
21. Church	.078

relationship denotes that the level of functioning for all sampled groups is similar. In other words, the subcategory Use of Church does not serve as an item that is diagnostic of family disorganization.

It should be noted that other subcategories with relatively low discriminatory power are: Source of income, Physical condition of the home, Informal associations, Job situation, and Use of most community resources except health agencies. This is to say, in the array of items that differentiate between adequate and problematic functioning, certain instrumental sets of behavior and social relationships beyond the family group appear to be less diagnostic of family disorganization than the bulk of intrafamilial relations and the sum total of behavior of the older family members.

Two Family Profiles

The following profiles of two families are presented to give the reader a comparison between a disorganized family, its historical pattern and the relationship of that pattern to the present family situation, and a family with a relatively organized pattern of family living. The two cases selected should not be taken as representing typical patterns of family well-functioning and malfunctioning. However, some of the characteristics of these two families, such as the nature of their solidarity and their patterns of communication, seem to be quite representative of the two polar groups studied.

One observation which can be made in the comparative analysis of levels of family functioning is that there is a general lack of family cohesiveness in the problem family, both between the parents and between the parents and children. Probably the clearest aspect of this situation, when the two profiles are compared, is the attitudes of the family members toward family integration. The problem family has a lesser degree of family solidarity; in addition, the behavioral components of the members' roles, that is, the dynamic aspects of the relationships, can be seen as blocking any attempt to "get together" as a family. The members appear to have established a set of interrelationships that furthers the disintegrating pattern and removes any possibility of communication and understanding within the family.

A further distinction between the two families is seen in their ability to cope with crisis situations. Both families have problems—financial, health, sexual, and so on. But the adequate family, in contrast to the problem family, is able to pull together and counter a stress situation with action or with an attitude affirming the primacy of family cohesiveness.

To be sure, this overly simplified conceptualization of multi-problem and stable behavior needs much further clarification of the mechanisms at work both within and outside the family group which contribute to the maintenance or disruption (and also the nonformation) of the family system. Nevertheless, within the broad range of total family functioning, the two profiles give comparable descriptions of a multi-problem and a stable family.

The selection of the two families was dictated in part by certain similarities that would permit a measure of comparability: two parents in the home, the same number of children (four) within a similar age range and the biological offspring of the family heads. Selection was also dictated by the availability of data for both families, covering present social functioning and background material on the families of procreation and also on the respective families of orientation. It should be noted that the multi-problem family is atypical in respect to the family's level of educational aspiration and the degree of formal social participation.

The presentations which follow are summaries of the interview records.

Multi-Problem Family

The Pumice family has no hope of solving its problems. Mrs. Pumice sees her role as one of simply trying to hold back the difficulties and crisis situations that have constantly accumulated since shortly after her marriage 23 years ago. The burden of responsibility for family affairs has fallen completely on Mrs. Pumice, as her husband has experienced a progressively debilitating illness affecting both his physical and his mental capabilities. His erratic behavior, stemming from the contraction of syphilis before marriage, has prevented him from assuming the traditional roles of breadwinner, husband, and father. He is constantly tormented by his children who view him as somewhat "crazy." Mrs. Pumice, also, takes out her frustrations on her husband in an overtly aggressive way. She feels her "bad" marriage is directly attributable to him and thus finds many opportunities to attack him through verbal abuse and by treating him like a child.

Mrs. Pumice also finds herself on the receiving end of aggressions from her four children. She has lost control of them. Mrs. Pumice has set high academic goals for her children stemming from the educational attitudes of her mother and father. These goals have been realized, in part, by her 21-year-old boy and 18-year-old daughter attending the local college. But the oldest boy, though quite academically efficient, has dropped out of college and has pursued other activities, thereby incurring many expenses which he expects his mother to meet. The younger girl wants to quit school and get married to her fiancé. The more Mrs. Pumice attempts to put across her point of view, the more recalcitrant and withdrawn the children become.

Reflecting on her life, Mrs. Pumice can recall only fleeting moments of accomplishment or happiness. She had 3 brothers and 3 sisters. Her father earned a salary of $12 a week in a factory, and they lived in a cold-water flat without electricity. The family seemed to be in a constant state of bickering. Her parents argued frequently and from Mrs. Pumice's observation were not happy with one another but stayed together out of the belief that a marriage once consummated must endure. She had a very poor relationship with her sisters who, to this day, attempt to control her life. Mrs. Pumice remembers few happy times during this period and summed up the lack of material goods, family cohesion, and warmth by saying, "We didn't have anything."

While she was in her middle twenties, Mrs. Pumice met her husband-to-be on a blind date arranged by her girl friend. Mr. Pumice, 29 years old at the time, appeared to her as handsome, masculine, and quite romantic. They carried on a steady 16-month relationship eventually leading to an 8-month formal engagement and a church wedding ceremony.

Certain situations developed during the premarital relationship that helped Mrs. Pumice to come to decisions that led to matrimony. Her mother died and Mrs. Pumice found herself completely supporting her aged father, since her brothers and sisters refused to give financial assistance. She vacillated for a time between her obligation to her family and Mr. Pumice's demands that they elope as he was "mad to marry me." She saw marriage as a partial escape from her family of orientation and their dictatorial attitude toward her. Her father was decidedly against the marriage because he felt that Mr. Pumice was a conniver, lazy, and would not adequately support his daughter. But the overriding concern to escape from the repressive life she was leading and a love for Mr. Pumice with whom she thought a full life would blossom became the deciding factors in her final decision.

Mr. Pumice also came from a large family, with his mother as the dominating figure in the household. He had only a childhood remembrance of his father who died when he was fifteen. His mother bitterly fought the marriage, as she did the marriages of all her sons. She wanted her boys to stay close to her and saw their marriages as just more trouble and problems that could easily be avoided by staying single. She openly disliked and snubbed Mrs. Pumice during the engagement period, and this behavior was intensified after the marriage.

Once married, Mrs. Pumice "saw her mistake." She found

out things about her husband she professed not knowing previously. He was a "mama's boy" and spent most of his spare time with his mother, forcing Mrs. Pumice—since she was lonely and without friends—to retreat to her siblings and her father. Mr. Pumice's mother's notion that "nobody was good enough for her children" became a reverberating theme with Mr. Pumice through his actions by generally supporting his mother and ignoring his wife.

During this first year of marriage Mrs. Pumice learned that her husband had syphilis. He had cohabited with different women for short periods prior to meeting Mrs. Pumice. She felt that none of these affairs was serious and did not concern herself with them. This premarital sex pattern, though, continued into marriage. She discovered a few months after the wedding ceremony that he was indulging in an extramarital affair. He continually debunked her inability to respond in the sexual act and used this as a justification for his outside sexual interests. He called her a "cold woman." She felt a slight revulsion toward sex, admitting that her husband got all the enjoyment from coitus whereas she "couldn't be bothered" and felt no obligation to "please him." These factors, combined with his going out every evening "with the boys" and leaving her alone, and a lack of money and accompanying accumulation of bills became the source of much conflict and led to her determination after eight months to terminate the marriage. He had lost his WPA job shortly after marriage (in fact it was doubted by her father whether he actually held a job) and she took over the economic responsibility by working as a dressmaker for $15 per week. Her disillusionment made her regret the decision to get married. If she had to do it over again she would have remained a spinster. But her siblings and father refused to take her back or support her in her contention; so her plans were thwarted.

The first child was born about two years after the marriage and the other three at the fourth, sixth, and eleventh years of marriage. She had wanted a large family, about five children, but after her first child and the immediate realization of all the care and work involved in his upbringing she abruptly changed her thinking about having more children. She claims that the following three children were all "mistakes." The first child was enough.

The lapse of two years before initial conception can be accounted for by her husband's unemployment and her desire to continue working in order to support the family. As a result, they used contraceptives until it was found that her husband could be reinstated on WPA if she was declared pregnant. She carried her first child well and felt good physically. But when the baby arrived she "felt terrible." For the first five months there seemed to be nothing to live for and no one to whom she could turn for assistance. She felt completely strange to this new experience, with the dingy apartment and gloomy surroundings adding to her generally poor disposition. Her husband was indifferent to her pregnancy and to the baby. He made it quite clear that he was not interested in children and offered no assistance in caring for the baby. She viewed his refusal to attend a class for new fathers and reluctance to take on the father role as evidence that he "was not meant to be a father." Any help she received from him was seen as a victory on her part.

The marital difficulties as they emerged during the first years of the marriage continued and were compounded by crises and unresolved conflicts as the children were being added to the family. Community agencies were sought out over the years, such as Family Service and State Welfare, to discuss the recurring and persistent problems facing the family and to receive aid. There was some attempt on Mrs. Pumice's part to respond to this outside assistance, but most of the gains were short-lived. She has viewed this as an inability of those community agencies to help her out. The relationship, in general, between her and these services has been tenuous. Her reactions have fluctuated between accepting concrete aid and advice, and blaming the services for their inability to render capable and lasting assistance. Her relationships with social work institutions have been indeterminate, weak, and fragmented. There is fleeting concern with the over-all family problems. Crucial crises, arising from the persisting conflicts in the family, are responded to, instead, and are then followed by a relaxation of effort until the next crisis.

Mr. Pumice's ability to use outside assistance is sharply limited due to his progressively worsening mental condition. His speech is impaired and his ability to function in simple tasks is dulled as a result of general paresis. Both parents have very poor relationships with their children; and presently the situation is reversed, and the children ridicule their father. Mrs. Pumice has found it impossible to relate to her children in any manner. They continually fight among themselves, are outwardly ashamed and embarrassed by their father's condition and express their hostility by such invectives as "You are sick, why don't you die!" The mother has overtly given up on her children. She plays one off against the other, openly favoring the first offspring and expressing much sensitivity to all his actions.

Whereas the oldest boy and girl appear to have fairly high academic ability, the sixteen-year-old daughter is considered by her teachers as an average student who is defiant of most authority and wants to quit school and get a job. The youngest daughter, aged twelve, is considered as exceptionally bright, pleasant, and affectionate.

Although Mrs. Pumice is unable to handle her children emotionally, she shows much control and knowledge in her other roles within the household. The children always appear neat, clean, and well dressed; and her home and furnishings are kept in good order. She maintains a high standard of operation in this area with her husband and children. The family, as a whole, actively participates in peer groupings around the neighborhood. Both parents continue to associate with their respective relatives. Mrs. Pumice is also quite active in church affairs and organized activities in the neighborhood. The oldest boy and the sixteen-year-old girl join the mother in these activities to some extent.

Because of Mr. Pumice's incapacitation the family's financial problems have been taken up by social welfare agencies during the past five years. Considering the limited income, few budget problems have arisen although at times bills have accumulated because of inadequate managing.

Stable Family

Although there have been a few rough spots in their marriage during the last nineteen years, such as the persistent financial problem, the Granits feel that their relationship is fairly solid, all things considered. In general, Mrs. Granit views her husband as a "good man." He is proud and independent; he primarily focuses upon his wife and children and finds most of his satisfactions and social life, apart from his job, with his family. He rarely goes out with male friends and does not drink. In this respect, Mrs. Granit has similar likes and dislikes. Although a few of her friends visit her occasionally, she remains involved mostly in housework and care for the children and seldom leaves her home even on week ends. Both parents are friendly with a few neighbors, but they keep aloof from everyone in the neighborhood as they "don't want to get involved" in the lives of others. This attitude extends also to formal associations except that the family attends church when they have the opportunity. The one aspect of their relationship that has been and continues to be a source of friction between them involves Mrs. Granit's family.

The Granits met through Mrs. Granit's sister, and it was three years after this initial meeting that they started to date regularly. Only one year of age apart and in their late twenties, they dated for an eight-month period that included a formal engagement of four months' duration. During this time the Granits had an enjoyable acquaintanceship. There were no quarrels or premarital conflict and no separations during this period.

When they decided to marry, Mrs. Granit was keeping house for her father and brother, and Mr. Granit was working regularly as a trucker. Mrs. Granit always viewed her husband as a good marriage prospect and "home fellow." When she saw all her brothers getting married and when the prospect of remaining a "servant girl" in her family started to bear down on her, she accepted his proposal. Shortly after marriage Mr. Granit was drafted into the Army, and his wife went to live with her father. Her mother had died when she was nineteen. Her father viewed the marriage favorably, since to his thinking nothing had changed; his daughter continued to live with him and to take care of his house.

During the first year of marriage, when her husband was in military service, Mrs. Granit experienced long periods of anxiety and loneliness. It was at this time that she faced many problems. Her husband's parents were dead and although she was on good terms with her sister-in-law she had no other close relationships with anyone. Her father and siblings never gave her any emotional support. Although she saw the many problems in her brothers' marriages, and thus had no illusion about marriage and saw it as "hard work," she did not expect it to be as difficult as it became for her. During the first year of marriage, as well as after, there were financial difficulties in addition to the problems presented to her by her family of orientation. Her feeling that she had no one to depend upon, and the negative attitude of her brothers and sisters, gave her a feeling of insecurity and rejection.

When she became pregnant shortly after marriage she "went wild." Her husband's allotment check was being held up, and with her general feeling of helplessness and isolation her pregnancy became a dreary ordeal. Shortly before the baby came Mr. Granit was discharged. They continued living with her father for the next three years. Along with the fact that Mrs. Granit continued being treated as a housemaid, her husband became embroiled with her family. She became angry at her family for expecting her to "wait hand and foot" on her father and at her husband for becoming increasingly belligerent about the whole situation. There was an eventual "blow-up," with the Granits moving out and setting up a household of their own. This move minimized the conflicted relationship but also started the financial problems since they now had to pay rent, buy furniture and household utensils.

In spite of these moments of bitterness, Mrs. Granit remembers her life with her family of orientation in a positive manner. As a large family they were poor and had very few material resources, but she recalls always having fun with her brothers and sisters. She was never close to her parents. Although she had dated a few other fellows before meeting her husband, she was never allowed to bring any of her boy friends into the home. Her parents told her nothing about the heterosexual relationship and she learned little about it until after marriage. Even as a child Mrs. Granit had ideas of eventually marrying. She conceived of having a large family, but the postmarital financial situation and difficulties in other areas forced her into a reconsideration of family size. But she continued to view marriage in a quasi-favorable way, remarking that life was full of problems whether one was married or not. Even though she has four children, eighteen- and sixteen-year-old boys, and twelve- and six-year-old girls, she has carried out a "planned" family mainly because of poor finances. Mr. Granit always wanted children and was quite pleased with the first baby, sharing the responsibilities of bringing up the child.

The sexual relationship between the parents did not commence until Mr. Granit came home on a short military leave a few months after marriage. At the time Mrs. Granit had difficulty connecting this event with her subsequent pregnancy. She placed little value on sex. Nonetheless there was a feeling of importance in the sharing of this part of marriage, and she followed through with her husband's desires quite willingly. As she saw it, it was obligatory in her role as wife, in that what was important for her husband was also of concern to her.

Both parents see the children as "coming first." All the central concerns in the family have immediacy in terms of the children. They willingly sacrifice for the children. Mrs. Granit never goes out and leaves them. She and her husband see to it that they keep away from potential trouble by bringing the children home after they have been out with their peers—and Mrs. Granit appropriately noted, "to do that you have to be home yourself." The children are punished by the father when they become troublesome. He does not hesitate to "strap the older boys" and he feels they must obey him "until they're married." Mrs. Granit leaves most of the discipline in the hands of her husband.

The financial situation takes primary position in the household. Social activities, clothes, and food are scarce as a result of their limited budget. Mr. Granit has a steady job which he has held for the past eighteen years, since his release from the Army. They plan regularly, but money management becomes one of "one week we rob Peter to pay Paul and the next week we rob Paul to pay Peter." Mrs. Granit sews in order to keep the children clothed. Although the children quarrel among themselves, the source of arguments does not center around the lack of material goods or their unequal distribution among the youngsters.

The children have presented very few large-scale problems to their parents. The oldest boy is attending a two-year college in the community where he expects to learn a skill for future job opportunities. The sixteen-year-old had rheumatic fever as a child but has no present complication. He continues to visit the clinic for a yearly checkup. The Granits view medical attention with favor, but feel restricted using doctors and dentists regularly because of a fear of mounting bills. The boy is of present concern to his parents because, although rated as a good student with college ability, he has recently slacked off in his school work, with resultant poor grades. Both younger girls are considered quite bright and active. The parents are proud of their scholastic accomplishments, for they hold education in high esteem.

Mrs. Granit prides herself on being "independent" and able to handle whatever family problems arise. She is aware of the function of social agencies in this respect and, except for some limited and rather disheartening experiences on her part, the family has never depended upon community assistance. They do make use of the dental and pediatric clinics but still retain a family doctor. To the extent to which they can keep family concerns to themselves, they do so. There is a mixture of anger at welfare agencies for not assisting during times of stress, but also a proud realization that they have never relied upon such assistance, but instead have seen the problem through and resolved it as best they could.

NOTES FOR CHAPTER 4

[1] A synopsis of this study appeared in the section "Articles in Brief" of *Marriage and Family Living*, Vol. 24, No. 4, Nov., 1963.

[2] Ernest R. Mowrer, *Family Disorganization* (Chicago: University of Chicago Press, 1927).

[3] Jessie Bernard, *Remarriage* (New York: Dryden Press, 1956).

[4] Reuben Hill, *Families Under Stress* (New York: Harper & Brothers, 1949).

[5] Ruth Cavan and Katherine Ranck, *The Family and the Depression* (Chicago: University of Chicago Press, 1938).

[6] Mirra Komarovsky, *The Unemployed Man and His Family* (New York: Dryden Press, 1940).

[7] For a typology of five kinds of family disorganization considering external and internal forces on the family system, see William J. Goode, "Family Disorganization," in R. K. Merton and R. A. Nisbet, eds., *Contemporary Social Problems* (New York: Harcourt, Brace & World, Inc., 1961), p. 390.

[8] E. E. LeMasters, "Parenthood as Crisis," *Marriage and Family Living*, 19, 353-355.

[9] Some selected sources include:

E. E. Atwater, *History of the City of New Haven* (New York: W. W. Munsell and Company, 1887).

R. G. Osterweis, *Three Centuries of New Haven: 1638-1938* (New Haven: Yale University Press, 1953).

R. A. Warner, *New Haven Negroes: A Social History* (New Haven: Yale University Press, 1940).

T. A. Dries, *A Handbook of Social Statistics of New Haven* (New Haven: Yale University Press, 1936).

[10] Herbert J. Gans, *The Urban Villagers, Group and Class in the Life of Italian-Americans* (Glencoe, Ill.: The Free Press, 1962).

[11] The contents of this section headed "Obtaining the Data" are cited or summarized from *Social Work* with permission of the editor. See Ludwig L. Geismar and Michael A. La Sorte, "Research Interviewing with Low-Income Families," *Social Work*, Vol. 8, No. 2, April, 1963 (New York: National Association of Social Workers), pp. 10-14.

[12] See especially the evidence presented in L. L. Geismar, *Family Diagnosis Similarity and Variance in Different Settings* (Rutgers, N.J.: Graduate School of Social Work, Rutgers—The State University, 1962, unpublished paper, mimeographed), p. 15.

[13] Epidemiological studies relating crisis situations to the occurrence of tuberculosis are especially suggestive in this connection. See John Cassel, *The Potentialities and Limitations of Epidemiology*. Paper read at the Seminar on Public Health for Schools of Social Work, March 4-9, 1962, Princeton, N.J., mimeographed.

[14] For a systematic account of the relative strengths and weaknesses of

experimental designs in sociology see Ernest Greenwood, *Experimental Sociology: Study in Method* (New York: King's Crown Press, 1945).

[15] See Geismar and Ayres, *Measuring Family Functioning* (St. Paul, Minn.: Family Centered Project, 1960).

[16] See Geismar, La Sorte, and Ayres, "Measuring Family Disorganization," *Marriage and Family Living,* Vol. 24, No. 1, Feb., 1962, pp. 51-56.

[17] Paul F. Lazarsfeld and Morris Rosenberg, "Comparison and Evaluation of Indices," in P. F. Lazarsfeld, ed., *The Language of Social Research* (Glencoe, Ill.: The Free Press, 1955).

[18] For similar findings for the St. Paul sample of 150 disorganized families using the Guttman scale analysis technique, see L. L. Geismar, Michael A. La Sorte, and Beverly Ayres, "Measuring Family Disorganization," *op. cit.,* Note 16 above.

CHAPTER  5:

BACKGROUND FACTORS
ASSOCIATED WITH
FAMILY DISORGANIZATION

In this chapter we shall discuss the second aspect of the total research on the 75 families, namely, an analysis of background factors and their association with present functioning patterns. As has already been noted, many approaches have been taken in previous studies of family disorganization. Most of them, though varying in emphasis, range within a socio-psychological framework. The disorganization of the family is viewed as primarily social in nature, and the background factors are also viewed as emanating from social interaction. In the present study, seven of the eight family functioning categories used to describe the present behavior of family members are concerned with the sociological content of family interaction. Only the category *Individual Behavior and Adjustment* contains what might be considered as psychological dimensions of personality behavior. This category comprises data pertaining to the mental and physical states and the role behaviors of the family members, with emphasis on the psychological component. Though it is directed toward psychological variables, the category represents a summation of role behavior in the other seven categories. Hence, the family profile takes a direction based chiefly on sociological variables.[1]

In asking what factors in the family history are "relevant" to a consideration of correlates of disorganization, the first concern is with the social context of family interaction, and the second is with the factors seen as being of importance in gaining a better understanding of family behavior.

Past research has employed factors which can be placed into two broad groups differing in degree and precision of measurement: demographic and attitudinal variables. The demographic variables, which are usually easier to gather and analyze, include age, sex, dates of events, et cetera; the attitudinal variables involve indices of behavior in which the subjective responses of the interviewee to any one aspect of family behavior are documented and later categorized as to content and frequency. In the present research, the variables to be studied were chosen on the basis of their relevancy in the framework of the two concerns noted above. In addition, special emphasis was given to those variables which discriminate by level of functioning. It should be noted that there are limitations to the use of retrospective data, inherent in the time lag between the study itself and the event, and in the difficulty seemingly experienced by the respondents in recalling happenings other than those associated with landmarks in the life cycle, such as marriage and birth of the first child.

Thus the data analysis took the following form:

The three subgroups of families, differentiated by their patterns of family functioning (Highs, Medians, and Lows), were cross-tabulated by the variables (40 in number) representing early antecedents to present social functioning. The frequency of occurrence (as against nonoccurrence) of each variable by family subgroup was determined on a percentage basis. Special attention was given to factors showing a linear relationship to present family malfunctioning and to a difference between Highs and Lows that by inspection appears substantial. The discovery of associations between antecedent patterns of behavior and present well-functioning and malfunctioning, it is assumed, will provide leads to a formulation of hypotheses on the processes leading to family disorganization. These hypotheses must be tested by longitudinal research.

The background variables fall into two classes: (1) the premarital variables, or those factors related to the couples that were operative before their marriages, and (2) the postmarital variables predominantly within the first year of marriage or up to the birth of the first child. The two classes are further subdivided into sets of variables appropriate to certain relationship and time categories. These sets of variables are presented below in the following order:

Premarital Variables
1. Family of Orientation
2. The Acquaintance-Engagement Period
3. Sexual and Attitudinal Conditions of Wife at Marriage
4. Demographic Characteristics of Parents at Time of Marriage

Postmarital Variables
1. Financial Status and Residence in First Month of Marriage
2. Satisfaction in the Marriage Relationship
3. The Sexual Relationship

4. Variables Relating to the First-Born Child
5. Child Spacing

The focus of the analysis is essentially in terms of variables associated with the Low, or malfunctioning, subgroup. All the excerpts of qualitative data presented are taken from interviews with families in the Low group. These excerpts point up the underlying attitudes, actions, and behavioral patterns peculiar to the Low families that are indicated by the percentage differences.

PREMARITAL VARIABLES

Family of Orientation

MARITAL RELATIONSHIPS OF COUPLES' PARENTS. Five areas of family behavior centering about the respondents' mothers and fathers and the wife's childhood were explored. The most singular difference among the subsamples was the husband's parents' marital relationship while he was still a part of his family of orientation. The families in the High group seemingly experienced a much greater amount of continued family solidarity than the problem families. (See Table 7.)

TABLE 7. PREMARITAL VARIABLES: PARENTS' FAMILY OF ORIENTATION (IN PERCENTAGES)

	High	Median	Low
Husband's parents never separated	81	67	38
Wife's parents never separated	69	62	54
Wife's parents' acceptance of marriage	48	41	36
Wife happy as a child	52	33	38
Husband's parents' acceptance of marriage	44	27	58

Temporary separations with previous conflict situations between the parents and unmarried motherhood rather than legal separation and divorce constituted the characteristic pattern of broken families of orientation. Separations occurred because of basic conflicts between parents usually involving drinking, extramarital affairs, and nonresolved problems relating to the children. One interviewer describes an eventual separation after a long duration of conflict centering about child rearing:

> Four or five years ago the husband's father left his wife because of her continued overprotection of her grown sons. She was always "bailing them out" of trouble. They could do no wrong and he could not take it anymore. Previous to that time there was no breakup, but there were many arguments about the proper way to raise the children.

But there were also relationships, though they were stormy throughout the marriage, that continued to persist within the marriage context:

> Both parents are alcoholics who frequently fought in a violent manner in front of the children. The marriage continued to exist even though [the respondent] recalls no moments of peace.

Two of the respondents had little or no home life or had no recollection of their biological parents ever being married. One husband stated:

> No, my parents were not married. I don't think they ever lived together. I must have been a mistake.

In another instance the husband was born out of wedlock, but later was reunited with his mother:

> The respondent was unable to give much information on his background, but he was probably illegitimate. He was in a foster home from the age of 3 and eventually returned to his mother and stepfather in his early teens.

Although the differentiation between the problem and stable families in respect to the wife's parents' marital status was not so large as that for the husband's parents (see Table 7), the wife's parents also experienced similar marital difficulties. Drinking and extramarital affairs predominated:

> They were never separated but both of them ran around. There were many arguments on my father's drinking.

> Yes, my parents were divorced. My father was a drinker and would beat my mother. He spent most of the money on drinks.

It can be noted that although conflict was persistent, the relationship between the parents was not necessarily a thoroughly negative one. The interviewer in paraphrasing the wife's response writes:

> Her parents broke up and separated when she was in her late teens. She was the youngest child. The separation was caused by her mother's continued objection to her husband's drinking. However, they separated without bitterness and at present visit each other. In fact her mother is about to move into a room in her father's house—as a tenant only—after a separation of 14 years.

The parents of the problem-family respondents had married lives that in many respects were not too different from the marital experiences of their offspring. Compatibility in marriage for most of the parents was a tenuous affair at best. This was also true for the respondents. Most of the conflicts in the respondents' parents' marriages emerged, it appears, as a result of specific concerns, such as a reaction by the wife against her husband's drinking and other outside activities, as well as a rather vague instability which stemmed from a lack of ability to resolve conflicts in the home. One area of disagreement easily led to a general set of conflicts between the parents that eventually took on a tone of bitterness and over-all reluctance to reduce the conflict. Although some of the parents inevitably withdrew from marriage, which can be taken as one mechanism of resolvement, other parents "stuck it out" even though one or both were clearly unhappy:

> My father always drank and spent money carelessly. There were a lot of arguments and mother threatened often to leave him but she never did.

PARENTS' ATTITUDE TOWARD THE MARRIAGE. From the respondents' replies, it appears that marriage in all three groups were not cordially accepted by the parents, and that most of their parents did not give their blessing to the impending marriage. Among the husbands' parents there seemed to be no discernible trend of acceptance or rejection of the marriage by level of functioning (Table 7). In less than half of all 75 families the parents looked somewhat askance at the marriage, and among many the attitudes of the parents were not known or were of such a placid nature that they were not considered as concerned, on the whole, about the marriage or their son's future wife.

On the other hand, the wife's parents took a much more critical view of the coming marriage. Only 36 per cent of the problem wives reported that there was general acceptance of their marriages, and about half of the parents of the well-functioning families voiced serious reservations about the daughter's marriage. Both father and mother took a stand on the marriage, with the mother apparently slightly more involved and vociferous about her daughter's future husband. The chief reason for rejecting the husband-to-be was his behavior and the parents' feelings about his marital possibilities in the light of this behavior. In one case both of the wife's parents objected strenuously to the chosen mate because of his

> . . . heavy drinking and explosive temper—especially after he broke the jaw of his wife's brother-in-law during the courtship.

Rejection of the fiancé by the parents was also based on

information about his activities quite apart from the relationship with their daughter:

My father warned me against him because he knew of his background as a gambler and drinker. He didn't want us to marry so we eloped (mother deceased).

Her mother was against the marriage because she knew he stole and didn't think he was good enough for her. Her father died before her marriage but he liked him. They drank together.

The mother objected also to her daughter's fiancé on rather vague, subjective, and intuitive grounds and warned her daughter of the consequences:

My mother didn't like him. She had a sense about people. She said he was sneaky and she didn't like his hovering mother who was always interfering.

Mother was against the marriage. She didn't like [my husband]. She told me that I was making a bad decision to marry him.

Another and less frequent reason for parental rejection was based on the age status of the daughter and her relationship to the family of orientation. The mother exerted the most pressure on the daughter in these cases and was rather persistent although not persuasive in wanting to keep the daughter single:

Her father was dead. Her mother felt that she was too young although another sister had married at age 15. "Mother wanted to hang onto me because I was the baby of the family."

This same kind of concern appears on the parents' part in this description of the evolving and changing parental attitude over time:

Her parents refused to accompany them to North Carolina where they got married. Her parents told her not to leave school but to wait until she was older. They were very angry when she went ahead with her plans. They did not prevent them from getting married in spite of their strong feelings. After the marriage her mother was very happy for them. The father was indifferent. Her mother felt that she knew what was best for her children and that her children should listen to what she had to say and act accordingly.

WIFE'S CHILDHOOD. The wives were asked what their childhood was like, that is, the nature of the relationships with their parents and siblings. The results show no clear relationship to malfunctioning (Table 7). The Low group of wives as well as the Medians saw their childhood generally as an unhappy period, and only slightly under one-half of the High group of wives experienced unhappiness.

The respondents were asked to give the interviewer some general notions of things which were satisfying and dissatisfying to them during their childhood. No attempt was made to reveal in depth any particular familial interaction or other relationship. The unhappy responses tended to focus on self-evaluation as a person in a family setting, parental dislike, and hard work as a child. The most frequent cause of unhappiness was the respondent's awareness that she either lacked something that was desirable or possessed a characteristic that was perceived as undesirable. One wife emphasized her unhappiness as a result of isolation and personal appearance:

My mother didn't love me and my brothers didn't either. I felt ugly and unwanted by everyone.

A feeling of inferiority also pervaded this respondent's youth because of her difficulty in vocal expression:

She began to stutter at the outset of puberty. She felt that this caused her unhappiness. But she sensed that she was happier than some of her siblings because she was the baby of the family and her father's favorite.

Another looked upon her existence as completely unhappy because she had no family of orientation:

She felt cheated that she did not have any parents or a family of her own. She lived in many foster homes but never felt that she was accepted as a part of the family. She felt that her family was only interested in her ability to work around the house. Her mother died when the respondent was 5 years old. Thereafter her father remarried and turned her over to the state for placement. She knows she has a brother someplace but has had no contact with either father or brother since her fifth birthday.

Economic deprivation was apparently not of major importance in determining the child's unhappiness as a member of the family of orientation. The lack of playthings, and of clothes and the like for the adolescent appeared to be consequences of tight budgeting, and, on the whole, these families had little money to spend on their children. Yet, economic deprivation does not appear as an overt determinate leading to unhappiness. In the following, lack of money is evident, but the nature of the relations in the family appears to take precedence:

There were seven children in the family and her father earned $12 a week. They had a three-room cold-water flat and no lights. Her parents fought constantly. Her father was ill-tempered and gave her mother a hard time. Her mother was a nice person but had to work too hard. The children fought all the time too. She remembers few happy times and said, "We didn't have anything."

"We didn't have anything" refers partly to the economic situation but also to the complete absence of family cohesiveness.

Compared to this general dissatisfaction, some sources of unhappiness occurred through the behavior of single family members. The following excerpts illustrate this point:

I was unhappy because I was ashamed of my mother. She got fits on the street and that embarrassed me. [The mother indulged in much outside sexual activity as well as probably being epileptic.]

Her parents had many fights and fought like animals. She didn't respect her father and slapped him once. He tried to molest her several times. He would walk around the house unclothed and she did not like that. Once he came home drunk and took his gun and started shooting at the statue of the Virgin. Things like this happened all the time. Her parents finally separated when she was 14 years of age. She remembers no happy times.

Connected with the notion of economic deprivation were the work patterns of some of the respondents as children. The following illustrations play down the economic necessity of work and emphasize, rather, deprivation from play activities because of child labor.

She laughed at the question and had a great deal of difficulty in answering. She asked me if I knew what it was like to pick cotton at the age of 7 or 8. She felt she had little time left for fun and play as there was so much work to do and everyone had to help.

She always had to work and give her father the wages which he immediately drank up. Her father would not allow her any freedom.

SUMMARY. Could it be that in a lower-class culture, where the man's behavior dominates the family picture, the kind of personality shaped by his home situation becomes a key factor in the life of the family he heads later on?

The parents' acceptance of marriage showed no consistent relationship to later disorganization. The husband's parents' acceptance, for reasons not clear to us, showed a trend toward a negative relationship; the wife's parents' acceptance a low positive relationship with later family stability. On the question of the parents' continued attitude toward the young couple, the data, though somewhat unsystematic, leave no room to suggest consistent differences between High and Low groups. In a few instances the parents remained an annoying factor in the marriage. In most of the problem families, as well as the nonproblem families, adaptation to the marriage took place, and problems in the later life of the young couple were not related to their families of orientation.

Among the premarital factors relating to the family of orientation, only the degree of unity in the husband's parental home showed a strong relationship to social disorganization in the family of procreation.

The parents of the wife took an active role against the marriage during the engagement period; the mother, especially, was against the marriage of her daughter. The marriages, however, were culminated despite these negative attitudes. Over 60 per cent of the problem-family marriages started out in such an atmosphere. The husband's inimical behavior was emphasized by the disapproving parents. Moreover, where the parents were in favor of the marriage the evaluation of the husband's personality was also a determining factor. Marriage itself as an institution was not a subject of concern to most parents. Although they themselves hardly experienced marital bliss, there was little evidence of a disparaging attitude toward marriage voiced in couples' presence.

The problem wives experienced slightly more unhappiness as children than the nonproblem wives. The instances the former cited were mainly within the context of family living: nonacceptance by parents and siblings and a sense of a lack of family solidarity that they apparently desired. Parental arguments were disconcerting and had reverberations upon the entire family. It is of interest that the wives focused on the family in reply to the question, "Were you happy as a child," although the question was not particularly centered on "family" happiness. Little mention is made of relationships outside the family, such as peer groupings and school.

Nonproblem wives showed more of a tendency to talk about peers and school, but family relationships remained the central focus.

The Acquaintance-Engagement Period

HOW AND WHERE THE COUPLES MET. The couples first made each other's acquaintance in a variety of ways, which can be grouped under three main headings: through introduction by a third person, informally by the male introducing himself to the female, and through an acquaintanceship that extended back to their childhood and grammar school days.

The most common method of meeting for the three subgroups was by introduction. In most cases the third person involved in bringing the couple together was a friend or relative, usually the female's, and the setting was either a party or a work situation:

> They were introduced by her girl friend at a New Year's Eve party. They began dancing and talking at once. He later asked her for another date.

> The respondent's sister introduced her to her prospective husband in the cleaning establishment where he and the sister worked. He later approached her for a date at their third meeting at a dance where he was a paid musician.

The informal meetings usually took place in the street or at a dance [2] and in some cases in a work or neighborhood setting. One wife's response to the sequence of events leading up to the eventual dating pattern is described by the interviewer:

> The respondent was a member of a small group of five girls who spent much time together usually walking around in the streets. One day the group engaged in a conversation with her husband-to-be while he was hanging around by himself. After

that, gangs of boys and girls mixed for a while. The respondent played the field of eligibles and finally settled on her husband who at that time was in the armed forces and in uniform.

Childhood acquaintanceships that lead to marriage either by the couple going together regularly for a number of years or in a sporadic fashion, are of interest since this occurred most frequently among the High group couples (Table 8). In contrast to this observed difference between levels of functioning, the patterns of meeting and the social settings in which the couples met have a proportionately similar frequency for the three subgroups. A High group couple and a Low group couple were likely to have met under the same set of circumstances.[3]

LENGTH OF ACQUAINTANCE AND ENGAGEMENT. As Table 8 shows, the High group couples knew each other for a longer period before marriage than the Low group couples. This can be accounted for partly by the greater proportion of Highs who were acquainted from childhood; it also represents a generally longer acquaintanceship even if they met as adults.

This point is evident especially in the longer formal engagements by the High couples. Formal engagement for the total sample of 75 families was 51 per cent. This is lower than the Hollingshead and Redlich finding of 70 per cent in a random sample of Class V families.[4] In some researches

TABLE 8. PREMARITAL VARIABLES: THE ACQUAINTANCE-
ENGAGEMENT PERIOD (IN PERCENTAGES)

	High	Median	Low
Little or no conflict during acquaintanceship	88	72	67
Acquainted over 2 years before marriage	59	24	38
Parents were acquainted from childhood	30	05	12
Engaged 7 months or more	60	42	45
Announced engagement	44	55	42

on lower-income couples, a pattern of drifting together with little conscious premarital planning seemed to be the rule.[5] In the present study, this pattern was apparent in only one or two instances. One respondent, in reply to the question of engagement:

> ... thought the question was amusing. She did not really know what was meant by an engagement period. The concept of engagement was difficult for her to comprehend nor did she feel it important or necessary.

NATURE OF THE ACQUAINTANCESHIP. The only acquaintance-engagement variable that revealed a definite linear relationship to problem functioning was the amount and kind of conflict experienced by the couple during the acquaintanceship period. Most couples in all three subgroups reported no conflict, but the High group had only three couples who got involved in some or much conflict as contrasted with eight Low-group couples.

The conflict among the Lows appeared to be much more intensified and focused mainly upon the male's behavior. Frequent drinking and purported infidelity were the sources of the conflict. Despite continuous arguments and physical violence, some couples stayed together throughout the acquaintance period, going from one argument to another:

> At first she painted their courtship as a happy time free of arguments. However on elaboration I learned that there had been many fist fights between them, each accusing the other of running around. Drinking was always a problem for them. When drunk they both became increasingly hostile. The fights were patched up by the female, a capitulation which she resented. "He has always been stubborn and pigheaded and could never admit he was wrong."

In some cases the arguments caused a breakup in the relationship, but the separation was usually of short duration. Nevertheless, reconciliation did not seem indicative of a resolution of the previous troubles between the couple:

During the 24 months of courtship and 12-month engagement there were frequent quarrels and occasional periods of breakup shortly followed by a making-up session. He would seem to tire of his relationship with her and turned to his male peer group for companionship—usually with beer drinking taking place. Then he would either run out of money or end up in jail for fighting. She would feel sorry for him and although fearful of his violent threats would take him back. There were always occasional arguments over his suspicious attitude toward her alleged activities with other men.

SUMMARY. The set of variables explored in this section show some differences between subsamples, but on the whole the distinctions are not clear cut. Only the nature of the acquaintance period gives some definite information on basic behavioral characteristics of the male partner. More will be said about this in the discussion below on the marital relationship in the first year of marriage. The length of time the couples associated varies somewhat with level of functioning. The getting-to-know each other period of the problem couples was not only pervaded by greater conflict and unresolved differences; it was also of shorter duration than the nonproblem couples. The average was 45 months for the High couples. Engagement remains a common experience which cross-cuts the subsamples. Using engagement as an indicator of premarital preparation and planning composed of a set of more or less vague expectations, the data do not support the contention that the couples "drifted" together into marriage in a rather haphazard manner.

Sexual and Attitudinal Conditions of Wife
  at Marriage

PREMARITAL PREGNANCY AND SEXUAL AWARENESS. The decisions made by the couples leading up to, and ultimately resulting in, marriage were usually clearly stated by the respondents. The problem wives felt that the precipitating factors in getting married were decisions made primarily between them and their husbands and to a lesser extent between them and members of their family of orientation. Much the same pattern appeared for the nonproblem families except that in some instances friends of both parties were instrumental in "encouraging" them to marry.

The type of interaction that went on between man-wife and wife-family which helped to lead to the marriage ceremony varied in kind, but the one factor that comes to the surface in the problem group is that of premarital pregnancy and the reactions to it.

Fifty-eight per cent of the Low or problem wives as against 45 per cent and 22 per cent of wives in the Median and High families, respectively, experienced premarital conception. (See Table 9.) The entire sample experienced 41 per cent premarital pregnancy.[6] Of these, 31 per cent gave birth before marriage. Pregnancy or the presence of an out-of-wedlock child appeared as a factor in the marriage in about one-half of these cases.

In some cases when it was discovered that the woman was pregnant her family issued the ultimatum to marry:

> I was seven months gone when I got married. My grandmother urged me to get married (when the pregnancy was revealed). I hesitated to do so, and my mother threw me out of the house. I went to South Carolina and worked 7 weeks as a chambermaid. After that I got married.

This type of parental pressure was evident when the wife was still living with her family of orientation. Premarital pregnancy, by itself a not uncommon situation among low-income groups,[7] was sometimes not the only impetus to marriage. The marginal nature of the family's economic standing and the desire to legitimize the child were forces which entered into the decision in many cases. An interviewer describes one response received:

> The overriding concern of the respondent was that she wanted a name for the child. Marriage did not particularly appeal to her nor did she love the man she married. She wanted to terminate her dependent status in her mother's home and establish a home of her own.

When a child had already been born and a marriage had not yet taken place, the precipitating factors leading to marriage were not necessarily the presence of the child. Often they were related to the couple's ability to "make it" in the marital setting financially and being successful in "getting along" with one another:

> She gave birth to his child eight months prior to their marriage. During her pregnancy they had thought of marriage but they could not agree on many things. He had no money to support a family and his drinking behavior bothered her. A few months prior to their marriage he secured employment at a saw mill. He saved his money, stopped drinking, and persuaded her that he could take care of her and the child.

TABLE 9. PREMARITAL VARIABLES: SEXUAL AND ATTITUDINAL
CONDITIONS OF WIFE AT MARRIAGE (IN PERCENTAGES)

	High	Median	Low
Child conceived before marriage	22	45	58
Wife saw marriage as fun-easy	54	61	85
Wife had much knowledge of sex	15	25	42
Pregnancy a deciding factor to marry	11	25	27
Peers as a source of sex knowledge	80	59	82
Wife wanted three or more children	27	36	27

Evasion tactics that attempted to lead the interviewer away from the area of premarital pregnancy as a factor in marrying were infrequently employed. Previous statistics on the first child's birthday and date of marriage were used to cross-check the premarital situation although most respondents readily admitted their pregnancies:

> Both had difficulty answering this question. They stated finally that they had thought of marriage for some time and both were looking for a marital partner. He felt in some ways he was lonely and that this led him into "the trap" of marriage. He had moved away from his family of orientation and was living by himself. Although she was probably pregnant at the time of marriage, they both avoided this in the discussion.

The traditional notion of the "forced" marriage, where premarital pregnancy is taken as the main determinant in marrying, can be assumed to apply only in some instances of premarital pregnancy (Table 9). The data suggest that the marriages must be looked at within the context of the couples' own social situation and not solely in terms of the wife's physical condition and the dictates of general, cultural mores:

> She was expecting a child but did not feel this would lead to marriage and went on to tell me about her husband. She stated that he had been living at home with his 72-year-old mother. He felt he was a burden to her as he had not been able to work for long periods of time. He suffered from epilepsy and in conjunction with this his wife felt that he might have fewer seizures if he married.

Correlated with the greater frequency of premarital pregnancy among the problem wives was a greater general knowledge of sex than among the stable wives. The frequency of premarital sexual experience was not recorded, but the knowledge of sex procured through carnal adventures was evident when pregnancy occurred:

> She learned by "hard experience" about sex as she had had an illegitimate son at the age of 16.

> She felt she knew a great deal about sex and just did not know how she got pregnant.

Sexual information for all three groups was obtained mainly through association with peers. It ranged from simply listening to the sexual escapades of the "other girls" to an active role in sexual play by the respondent:

> The girls talked about sex and the girls who were "fooling around knew a lot." Her sister and herself were the only ones in the crowd who did not fool around sexually.

> Her mother told her nothing. She picked up the information from other girls and started sex activity very young because "everybody else was doing it."

Their mothers and fathers provided them with little or no knowledge of sex:

> I didn't know nothing. It was considered a crime by my family. I couldn't even bring a fellow in the house.

Most of the wives had only superficial knowledge or none at all of the biological processes, and some who remained rather isolated from the "street talk" were completely ignorant of what sex was all about until marriage.[8]

PRECONCEPTION OF MARRIAGE AND FAMILY SIZE. The notions that the wife had of marriage before entering the marital partnership separated the problem subgroup from the other two quite dramatically. A full 85 per cent of the problem-family wives visualized marriage in a rosy, romantic, "it'll be swell" glow with little debate over possible "adjustments" and "problems" that would have to be overcome after marriage. Only about half of the wives of the stable families looked at marriage in these terms; the balance viewed it either as a "hard chore," as something which would have to be "worked out" and adapted to, or without any specific set of marital expectations.

The Low wives' expectations seemed to come quite close to the Hollywood conception of marriage: a state of bliss, glamour, and happiness. In the following excerpts the preconception of marriage emerges as the end of life as a developmental process and the beginning of a completely ecstatic and erotic existence:

> She thought being with him would be the "most wonderful thing in the world." It would be "like what you saw in the movies and everything would be fine."

> She thought marriage would be a "bowl of cherries."

> "Everything would be nice—peaches and cream."

> She had a romantic image of marriage and thought it was all "love and kisses."

The section below, on satisfaction in the marital relationship will deal with the degree to which these expectations were met.

Another question in this area concerned the respondent's wish for children at the time of marriage and her idea of an "appropriate" family size. As can be seen in Table 9, few wives in any of the subgroups wanted large families. The desired family size was about two children and in only five of the 75 cases did the wife specify that she wanted no family. Most wives had thoughts about children previous to marriage; ten respondents claimed they had not given it any consideration. The present size of all the families studied is quite different from these initial expectations of the desired size of the family. All mothers did eventually have at least one child and most of the families at present have three or more children. (It should be noted that one or more children was one of the selection criteria.) The median number of children by level of functioning is: High 3.31; Median 3.83; Low 4.40.

SUMMARY. The problem-family wives had more premarital pregnancies at the time of marriage than did the wives in the Median and High groups. The problem-family wives also appeared to know more about sex from their experience of pregnancy and childbearing than did the wives in the other two subgroups, but the wives in all the subgroups derived much of their initial sex knowledge and experience from peers.[9] The romantic image of marriage was much more predominant among the Lows than among the Medians and Highs. Few differences were noted in the wives' expectations regarding family size. Most of them eventually gave birth to more children than they had initially thought appropriate.

Demographic Characteristics of Parents at Time of Marriage

AGE AT MARRIAGE. In the early 1950's in New Haven the median age for marriage for Class V couples in the bottom socio-economic grouping in which the 75 sampled families belong was 23 for males and 19 for females.[10] The families in our own sample present a varied picture. The males' median age at marriage was 23. The Low-group male married later in life than the High-group male, with medians of 24 and 21 years of age, respectively. The median age for all wives was 20 with the Lows marrying at 19 and the Highs at 20. Almost 70 per cent of the Low males married when they were 23 or older (Table 10). This is in contrast to the 74 per cent of Highs who married when under 23 years of age. Using age 23 as a cut-off point, a slightly smaller proportion of Low wives than High wives married before 23. Age at marriage ranged for both male and female from 15 to 35 years or over.

Hollingshead's finding of a large age discrepancy between male and female in Class V is corroborated by the present data. Thirty-two per cent of the husbands in his random sample [11] were 6 or more years older than their wives as compared to 29 per cent of our sample. When our sample is broken down by level of functioning, it is evident that the age difference increases as the level of functioning decreases

(Table 10). Low couples are further apart in age, with wives marrying at approximately the same time as do most females in Class V and husbands somewhat later.

Multiple marriages might partly account for the husband's advanced age, but the evidence is not striking (Table 10). Some Median and Low husbands had been married previously, usually only once, with dissolution by divorce or death. However, Low husbands were much more likely to be marrying younger women even though many did not marry until after age 27.

No High-group husband had had a previous marriage, and fewer than one-fourth of the husbands in the lower functioning groups had been married more than once. Common-law attachments and long-term "shacking-up" appeared in only a few instances and were randomly distributed throughout the sample.

EDUCATIONAL STATUS. Previous researches have generally pointed out that the education factor parallels other socio-economic factors in the description of lower socio-economic groups.[12] Most of the inhabitants of this stratum rarely achieve an education equivalent to high school or beyond. Most of the 75 couples in the present study did not complete the elementary grades.[13]

The formal education of the families reveals no discernible differences among the subsamples (Table 10). The median education for males and females reaches the grammar school level, with only 30 to 40 per cent going beyond the ninth year. Lows as well as Medians and Highs were lower class by this criterion as well as by occupation and residence.

MARRIAGE SETTING. The Highs were more likely to be married in a church. Fifty-nine per cent of the High couples were thus married as compared to only 35 per cent of the Lows.[14] The Low ceremonies took place in the home, rented halls, a bar and grill, at an official's residence such as the home of a justice of the peace, or the city hall, with a justice of the peace as the usual officiator. In a few cases a minister performed the ceremony in these settings. Regardless of place of marriage, more Highs than Medians and Lows were married by clergymen as shown in Table 10.

SUMMARY. Husbands in the Low group married at an older age than husbands in the other two groups to wives whose age equaled that of the lower socio-economic median. The couples' age difference was pronounced with most males marrying after the age of 22. Most marriages were the couples' first. An eighth-grade graduation represented the normal scholastic attainment. The marriage ceremony took place predominantly outside the church setting, and was performed by a civil servant.

TABLE 10. PREMARITAL VARIABLES: AGE, EDUCATION, AND MARITAL STATUS AT TIME OF MARRIAGE AND WHERE MARRIED (IN PERCENTAGES)

	High	Median	Low
Husband under 23 years of age at marriage	74	32	31
Parents' age difference 6 years or more	15	32	42
Married in a church	59	43	35
Married by a clergyman	70	67	50
Husband's first marriage	100	76	80
Wife under 23 years of age at marriage	78	59	65
Husband: 9 years or less formal education	69	71	62
Wife's first marriage	100	91	96
Wife: 9 years or less formal education	67	68	65

POSTMARITAL VARIABLES

*Financial Status and Residence
in First Month of Marriage*

A "sufficient" amount of money to sustain an "appropriate" level of urban living varies from one family to another.

The financial resources that are available to the family at the beginning of the marriage, the family's budgeting pattern if any, its tastes and values and buying patterns regarding material objects, its consumption of alcoholic beverages, drugs and the like, these and other variables produce the highly subjective concept of a "sufficient" family income.

The material derived from the contemporary functioning patterns of the sample families provided a more objective set of data on the family's sufficiency of income and appropriateness of expenditure than data gathered about the situation at the beginning of the marriage. As this study had to rely on recall of behavior a number of years earlier it was possible only to ask for information pertinent to debts incurred and job employment during the year following establishment of the family.

TABLE 11. POSTMARITAL VARIABLES: FINANCIAL STATUS AND RESIDENCE IN FIRST MONTH OF MARRIAGE (IN PERCENTAGES)

	High	Median	Low
Heavy financial debt	07	09	27
Husband with steady employment	67	68	56
Neolocal residence	58	50	60
Wife working	48	36	19

As noted in Table 11, heavy financial debt at marriage was of low frequency for all families, but there is an almost fourfold increase from the High to the Low group. For the Low couples, incurring debt as a result of an accumulation of marital expenses such as buying furniture and clothing, was negligible. In most cases debts were more likely the result of excessive drinking or other forms of indulgence by the husband. Even though over half the couples lived apart from their respective parents or in-laws, initial expenditures were minimal as couples moved into furnished rooms or flats or sought other arrangements rather than buying total sets of furnishings for their homes. Several of those couples who moved in with a set of parents, primarily the wife's, made reference to the fact that not having to pay rent saved them from falling into serious debt.

Although most of the males in the sample held regular jobs at marriage all three groups showed low rates of steady employment. No couple was on relief at marriage. The Low group contained only slightly more males who either worked sporadically or were unemployed. Though the jobs held by the group—meat cutter, janitor, car washer, farm laborer, ditch digger, construction worker, trucker, saw mill worker —did not pay particularly high wages, the spending patterns often hinged upon the behavior of the male marked by inconsistent employment, gambling, and especially drinking. A drinking habit by the husband which consumed quite rapidly any income or savings appeared to be chiefly responsible for the couples' inability to pay for necessities, such as food, rent, and clothing, and for an accumulation of bills. In only a few cases did the family of orientation or friends help out financially through direct money loans.

The percentage of wives working at marriage clearly distinguishes the subgroups. Almost one-half of the High wives held jobs—full-time and part-time—as compared to only one-fifth of the Low wives. The more frequent occurrence of premarital and immediate postmarital pregnancy among the Low wives can account in part for the differential job situation.

SUMMARY. The sample as a whole revealed few couples who were in financial debt at marriage; but most of these couples were found within the Low group. Most males had steady employment at marriage. Heavy financial debt appeared to stem from the drinking habits of the males, a behavior which quickly turned a "marginal" income into one inadequate to fill basic needs. Supplementary earnings by the wife were least evident in the Low subsample. This finding parallels the present employment statuses of the families: the adult male remains the principal breadwinner in the problem families, with High families showing more diversification in role behavior in this respect. It is possible, however, that the difference in present functioning can be attributed to the fact that the High families are older and have somewhat older children, and hence may be in a better position to avail themselves of supplementary employment opportunities. This argument does not take into account the probable nexus between the nature of employment and the variance in overall social functioning among the sample groups.

Satisfaction in the Marital Relationship

The premarital expectations of the marriage relationship held by the Low wives—romance and happiness—were rudely shattered during the first year of marriage. The wives' reactions to their marriages varied widely, but most of the disappointments in the marriage centered around marital arguments and the husband's drinking:

> The first six months were fine. Then he started going out by himself and drinking. When I asked him where he'd been he'd beat me. He put me in the hospital twice. I became very afraid of him.

> I thought marriage would change my husband—stop his habit of drinking. He only got worse.

Some wives thought marriage would give them an opportunity to "escape" from tedious and obnoxious situations, but it seemed only to amplify them and bring the wife right back into relationships which she had disavowed:

> She wanted to own her own home and have a nice family. She found it was just the opposite. They always fought. The only thing her husband had was good looks. Marriage was not the cure-all she expected.

She had seen marriage as "getting away," not staying in the same town (or state), and doing something different. She had not given much thought to money and only too quickly realized how little they could do without it. She wanted to live in New York City, and going to the farm was a disappointment. She also desired to get away from home, and coming back to live with her parents also proved unrewarding.

CONFLICT AFTER MARRIAGE. Premarital conflict was apparent among the Low couples to a greater extent than among the others. After marriage the conflictual relationships spread to more families in the sample, and only 32 per cent of the Low wives reported little or no conflict in their marital relationships (Table 12). Most of the conflicts originated in the couple's lack of money to carry on everyday affairs, compounded by the husband's tendency to "drink the paycheck away" and the ensuing arguments:

They argued about money, about not having enough in the house and about his excessive drinking. He held no responsibility as a husband and completely ignored his obligations.

After they went to New York they began really fighting. He "kicked up," was an unsteady worker and thus got fired from his jobs for laziness so there was insufficient money. They were "eating off his mother" usually once a day.

As might be expected, the wives' satisfactions in marriage varied with the degree of conflict. The question which most

TABLE 12. POSTMARITAL VARIABLES: WIVES' SATISFACTION WITH THE MARITAL RELATIONSHIP IN THE FIRST YEAR (IN PERCENTAGES)

	High	Median	Low
Would have married again	75	65	47
Wife found marriage satisfactory	50	52	30
Little or no marital conflict	50	70	32
Happy marital relationship	64	68	50

vividly brought out the differences between the High, Median, and Low wives on how they perceived the marital relationship in the first year was, "Would you have done it over again?" (Table 12). Three-quarters of the High wives responded that on the whole they found marriage—which was construed by the wives to mean with their immediate mate and under the circumstances prevailing in the first year —a pretty good arrangement and had no regrets about the marriage. In contrast, less than one-half of the Low wives stated this. The Low wives were bitterly disappointed. The husbands proved to be rowdies, drank too much, ignored them, and they found out that "loving" them was impossible. Some wives focused upon the advent of pregnancy as a "shock" and defined marriage in relation to this experience. The Low wives' reactions to their marriages can be summed up by the way one wife responded to the query. She said, "Are you kidding?"

SUMMARY. General satisfaction in the first year of marriage for the wives was correlated in part with social functioning. The reasons for disappointment were usually quite specific and related to the disruption of premarital expectations and the argumentative nature of the relationship involving the husband's drinking and carousing. The result was lack of money and the inception of the wife's general tone of bitterness toward the entire marital relationship.

The Sexual Relationship

The sexual relationship in marriage was a rather one-sided affair for all the couples. In the main, the wives stated that their husbands desired and enjoyed sex more than they did throughout the marriage. These feelings, though one could argue that they represent the "expected" response by women, were a source of marital dissatisfaction and brought criticism of the husband's behavior.[15]

In some instances the husband proved to be quite demanding and ineffectual in satisfying his wife:

> Her husband would have orgasm and would pull out to go
> to sleep. He did not stay with "it" until she got enjoyment out
> of it.

> Her husband got the most enjoyment because it was painful
> for her. She did not have "sex" with him often but did indicate
> that she has enjoyed sexual relations with other men.

> He called her frigid and debased her sex ability. She came
> to the point where she "couldn't be bothered."

To other women the sex act would have represented an enjoyable experience had not the "danger" of pregnancy been
one of its consequences:

> She was fearful of pregnancy and only enjoyed sex after she
> became pregnant "with nothing to lose."

On the other hand, the wives who did enjoy sex saw themselves as much more desirous of coition than their husbands.

> For the first year she wanted sex all the time. However, she
> could not say she enjoyed it thoroughly because insertion hurt
> her. But she wanted it more than he did.

> He always said she was the sexy one. She reached the cli-
> max before he did.

When the respondents were asked whether they thought
that sex was an important part of their lives at the beginning
of marriage the Low wives were more prone to answer
affirmatively than the High wives. The Lows often viewed
sex in conjunction with their obligation as wives, and whatever their husband wanted they felt a duty to provide:

> She felt that it was important at first because her husband
> made demands on her and she wanted to keep him happy.

> . . . by having sexual intercourse with him she felt that she
> was making him happy.

The High wives, on the other hand, responded to this question mostly in terms of a desire for children and a family. In addition, the Highs had a broader range of "items" that were important in marriage. They were more likely to include companionship, having a home, socializing, and other goals which they felt marriage could bring to them. The Low wives' focus of a high value placed upon the sexual relationship appeared in some cases as a major element in the marriage, and the focal point in the understanding of why these individuals married and what they felt marriage was all about:

> She was vehement about this because she verbalizes sexual desire as the reason for marriage. This was important because sex provided a wonderful feeling, something new and something to look forward to.

> Sex was important and the first year she loved it. After that she considered it a duty.

> It was very important—the most important thing. Sometimes they would leave places they were visiting or movies so they could go home and have sex. This was fine with her. She was madly in love with him.

The Low wives' greater valuation of sex corresponded with a seemingly greater sophistication in this area prior to marriage (see Table 9). Despite the fact that the Low wives placed greater value on sex before and after marriage, they were somewhat less likely than the wives in the stable families to report sharing the joys of sexual experience with the husbands.

SUMMARY. With most couples, the sexual relationship was exclusively enjoyed and sought after by the male. Sexual compatibility was not a dominating characteristic of the couples during the first year of marriage in any of the three groups studied. In relation to a list of satisfactions that might be experienced in marriage, the Lows put greater emphasis on the importance of sex, whereas the Highs put greater stress on the value of children as well as other satisfactions that they sought from marriage and a family. A difference in basic values may be inferred from the greater emphasis placed by the Low wives upon receiving (sex) and a lesser emphasis upon giving [children].[16] (See Table 13.)

TABLE 13. POSTMARITAL VARIABLES: THE SEXUAL
RELATIONSHIPS (IN PERCENTAGES)

	High	Median	Low
High valuation placed on having children	48	17	16
High valuation placed on the sexual relationship by wife	35	50	63
Both partners enjoyed the sexual relationship	46	28	35

Reactions to the First-Born Child

Pregnancy and the approaching birth of the first child can be a joyous experience, one that the mother looks forward to, or it can be a period of deep remorse for the mother with feelings of rejection of the child and herself. When the wives were asked about their feelings toward the first pregnancy, the gestation period, and the eventual delivery of and care of the new-born, it was evident that the Low wives were more likely to be remorseful than joyous.

Over half the Low wives, as can be seen from Table 14, reacted negatively when they discovered they were with child. Fewer showed negative feelings during the period of pregnancy, and the number with negative feelings decreased steadily as gestation progressed. This trend held true for all three subsamples.

The Low wives who were negatively disposed to the child throughout pregnancy and birth were those who delivered out of wedlock. These wives became alarmed with the discovery of their condition. Carrying the child only served to maintain and sometimes increase the anxieties of the mother:

"I felt awful." She did not know the connection when she missed her period, but her mother noticed she had skipped and told her that she was going to have a baby. Her mother was hurt and rather mad, but attempted to alleviate her daughter's feelings. The entire family sympathized and supported her, but she felt ashamed and miserable and did not leave the house. When the baby came she was still miserable. Her mother took care of the baby for the first three years after which the respondent married and took the child.

Most of the Low wives' first reaction to pregnancy was negative, but their feelings changed when the baby finally arrived. A desire not to have children was one reason for the despondency:

She was very frightened when she became pregnant. She did not want children. The pregnancy was difficult and lonely partly because her husband was in the military at the time, and without many other social outlets she felt lonely for him. She stated she was happy when the baby girl arrived.

Pregnancy compounded by physical reactions gave some mothers second thoughts about having children:

She was surprised at becoming pregnant. "I didn't want it and felt pretty bad about it. I was real sick the whole time, with all of them. But I was pleased with the baby."

The attitude of not wanting children emerged frequently as a source of negative reaction to the pregnancy. In only a negligible number of cases was this a reaction to the husband's lack of desire for children; rather, the wives emphasized their own feelings on the subject:

She felt ashamed, afraid, and angry when she found out. She did not want to tell her parents as she was not sure what they would say and did not do so until the seventh month. She was angry with her husband and blamed him for her condition. She continued to be angry with him until the baby arrived. She was then so pleased with herself, the baby and her husband, that she allowed him to see her again.

With their median ages at 20, most of the wives were fairly young and inexperienced at the time of the first pregnancy and birth. Most pregnancies were either unexpected, and/or unwanted. Many wives were frightened at the thought of caring for a baby—something which they knew little about and felt they could not handle. Although only a minority of the husbands failed to express a desire for chil-

TABLE 14. POSTMARITAL VARIABLES: RELATING TO
FIRST-BORN CHILD (IN PERCENTAGES)

	High	Median	Low
Wife had negative reaction to pregnancy	40	45	58
Wife felt negative while pregnant	32	35	54
Wife felt negative toward new-born	12	20	33
Husband assisted new-born	65	59	55
Husband expressed desire for children	88	100	75

dren (Table 14), most of them, as well as the respective families of orientation, gave little or no assistance in the form of emotional support to the wives. The impression from the data is that the newness of the experience, general ignorance of the nature of pregnancy, a feeling that something was happening to them that they could not readily comprehend, and that would have unforeseeable consequences contributed to the dejected state of mind of the Low wives.

Once born, most neonates found acceptance not only by the mother but also by the fathers. For the sample, the majority of fathers assisted in the care of the baby either directly or by taking over other household chores when the mother was busy with the child. This behavior showed only a slight positive relationship to family functioning. High fathers were more likely to assist than Low fathers.

SUMMARY. The reaction to pregnancy and its aftermath

was found to be directly related to the problem families. Low mothers generally took a negative view of the experience. There was no evidence that the traditional dichotomy, thought to exist in low-income husband-wife role sets, was in operation.[17] Most male heads of families assisted in tasks generally identified with the wife-mother role in lower-class families.

Child Spacing

The birth dates of all children born to the families were recorded by the interviewer and cross-checked with factual data in the housing authority files. It was deemed desirable to find out whether any association appeared between problem functioning and the number of children born and when they were born during the marriage period. The relevant data are presented in Table 15. Only the first ten years of

TABLE 15. THE PRODUCTIVITY RATE IN THE FIRST TEN
YEARS OF MARRIAGE BY LEVEL OF FUNCTIONING

	High	Median	Low
Proportion of children in first ten years born in the:			
First Year *	10	11	28
First Five Years	53	57	72
Proportion of families having 3 or more children in the:			
First Five Years	19	32	46
First Ten Years	64	57	66

* Includes premarital pregnancy and out-of-wedlock.

marriage were considered, in order to include all the families.

Child spacing was found to vary directly with social malfunctioning. Not only did the disorganized families have one more child on the average than the stable families, but the first five years of marriage showed a disproportionately large number of births in the malfunctioning group. In the High group the children were more evenly spaced. More specifically, in ten years of marriage, the well-functioning families had ten per cent of the children born during the first year and 53 per cent by the fifth year. By contrast, the Lows had 28 per cent of the children born during the first year and 72 per cent by the fifth year. Thus by the fifth year of marriage the proportions of families with three or more children were: Highs 19, Medians 32, Lows 46 per cent. The first five years of marriage represented differential productivity among the groups, but by the tenth year family size tended to even out with about two-thirds of the sample having three or more children.

SUMMARY

In the present chapter we have attempted to pinpoint antecedent factors, occurring early in the family life cycle, which contribute to family malfunctioning. The primary object of this effort was an exploration of ways leading to early identification of multi-problem functioning. Our method of studying the problem utilized the ex post facto technique of proceeding from the phenomenon to be explained by a collection of earlier data which might have impinged upon the phenomenon. Information gathered was confined to sets of behavior and events which were associated with basic landmarks in the family life cycle, particularly courtship, marriage, and birth of the first child.

This selection was designed to reduce some of the hazards in the whole approach, which are inherent in the problem of recollecting events occurring in the more distant past. It was thought that occurrences associated with important turning points in life might be recalled with a greater degree of reliability than events taking place with no such anchorage in time. Furthermore, these landmarks in life constitute in themselves situations which are seen as influencing both the patterns of subsequent behavior and interactions of the family members. Despite these safeguards, it must be kept in mind that the approach of utilizing retrospective data has as its main goal the formulation of hypotheses for testing by more rigorous methods.

All the 75 families in the sample, divided by level of family functioning into three groups called High, Median, and Low, belonged by virtue of residence and occupation to the lower class. This fact was verified by the finding of limited formal education of the parents and a low rate of steady employment of fathers. Level of functioning showed very little relationship to these indices of social class.

A basic conclusion to be drawn from this study suggests that there are factors in the earlier life cycle which may differentiate stable from unstable families. These factors involve the behavior of the families of orientation and the early functioning of the families of procreation; for example, parents of heads of unstable families had experienced more marital disruption than parents of heads of stable families. The converging evidence from this analysis suggests that the home situation has an effect upon the children's subsequent functioning as marriage partners and parents.

The multi-problem families, in contrast to the more stable ones, were characterized by an early partnership between the man and the woman characterized by greater age differences, a shorter acquaintance before marriage, more conflict during the acquaintanceship period, more premarital pregnancies, fewer church weddings, and a more idealized, less realistic set of expectations regarding married life. Financial debts at the beginning of marriage were also more common among the poorly functioning families, and the husband's job pattern was characterized more often by intermittent unemployment. Fewer wives in the problem families assisted the family financially by going to work.

The first year of marriage in unstable families was marked by more extensive conflict than the beginning of married life in the stable ones. The more frequently expressed feelings of dissatisfaction by wives in unstable families may possibly be related to such marital conflict. Wives in malfunctioning families brought to the marriage more sexual sophistication and placed a higher value upon the sexual experience. There is no evidence, however, that this disposition made for better sexual adjustment in the low-functioning families; in fact, the evidence tends to be in the other direction.

Other differences, emerging early in the family career, and setting apart the stable from the multi-problem families, pertain to the values and expectations of parents. Wives in stable families placed a higher value upon having children and showed a more positive attitude toward pregnancy and toward the new-born than did the wives of problem families. The spacing of births differed substantially between the two groups, suggesting that more planning for children was done in the stable than in the disorganized families. It appears that the absence of realistic expectations and planning for the future is more characteristic of disorganized than adequately functioning families. A difference in basic values is suggested by a greater emphasis upon receiving (sex) and a relatively lesser emphasis upon giving (children), found in mothers of the problem families. These characteristics possibly tied to earlier socialization processes and leaving their mark upon the personality, may represent a set of psychosocial forces which run through the whole family life cycle. They might be seen to underlie later family functioning marked by inability to meet the need of its members.

A characteristic sharply distinguishing the disorganized from the more stable families is the age of the family group and, correlatively, the family's life cycle stage. Problem families were found to be younger with fewer of the children out of the home and independent. This observation corresponds to the findings of Charles V. Willie of Syracuse who also compared stable and problem families in a low-cost public housing project.[18]

The nature and size of the sample precludes any attempt to explore the effect of such factors as population mobility and housing authority policy upon the age distribution of families. However, this should be done, since there is the possibility that the age difference is not spurious but actually does differentiate between stable and unstable families. If so, the question arises whether the period of family instability is confined to certain life cycle stages. Is there a saturation point to social disorganization giving rise to a bipolar development in family functioning? Do families after years of conflict and instability either stabilize or fall apart? Such an hypothesis does not contradict another tentative conclusion of this study that disorganization begets disorganization. It is possible that multi-problem families which survive their trials and tribulations may become stabilized after most of their children have been launched on a shaky career of their own.

NOTES FOR CHAPTER 5

[1] Other research designs which assess family disorders in a clinical setting and are mainly made up of psychological variables with a personality approach can be found in the following works: N. W. Ackerman, *The Psychodynamics of Family Life* (New York: Basic Books, Inc., 1958); Erika Chance, *Families in Treatment* (New York: Basic Books, Inc., 1959); J. M. Hunt and L. S. Kogan, *Measuring Results in Social Casework* (New York: Family Service Association of America, 1950).

[2] Hollingshead and Redlich report similar patterns of meeting for Class V. See August B. Hollingshead and F. C. Redlich, *Social Class and Mental Illness* (New York: John Wiley & Sons, Inc., 1958), p. 126.

[3] The initial phases of the relationship, the meeting and social setting, may vary among social classes. See John E. Mayer, *Jewish and Gentile Courtships* (Glencoe, Ill.: The Free Press, 1961), pp. 33-37; Clark E. Vincent, *Unmarried Mothers* (Glencoe, Ill.: The Free Press, 1961), pp. 88-91; Hollingshead and Redlich, *op. cit.*, pp. 126-127.

[4] Hollingshead and Redlich, *op. cit.*, p. 126.

[5] Lee Rainwater, *And the Poor Get Children* (Chicago: Quadrangle Books, Inc., 1960), pp. 62-63.

[6] This approximates Hollingshead's finding of 40 per cent in Class V from a random sample. See Hollingshead and Redlich, *op. cit.*, p. 126.

[7] The literature on the incidence of illegitimacy and its differential frequency among the socio-economic classes is voluminous. See Clark E. Vincent, *Unmarried Mothers* (Glencoe, Ill.: The Free Press, 1961), Chs. 1 and 3, pp. 291-302.

[8] Rainwater, *op. cit.*, p. 63. The lower-class pattern of sexual knowledge described here appears similar in content. Also see Lee Rainwater, Richard P. Coleman, and Gerald Handel, *Workingman's Wife: Her Personality, World, and Life Style* (New York: Oceana Publications, 1959).

[9] For a view of similar premarital sexuality and sex instruction of lower-class Jamaican women, see Judith Blake, *Family Structure in Jamaica* (Glencoe, Ill.: The Free Press, 1961), Ch. 3.

[10] Hollingshead and Redlich, *op. cit.*, p. 126.

[11] Hollingshead and Redlich, *op. cit.*, p. 126. See also August B. Hollingshead "Cultural Factors in the Selection of Marriage Mates," *American Sociological Review*, Vol. 15, No. 5, Oct., 1950, pp. 619-627, particularly p. 622.

[12] Jerome K. Myers and B. H. Roberts, *Family and Class Dynamics in Mental Illness* (New York: John Wiley & Sons, Inc., 1959), pp. 24-26. Rainwater, *op. cit.*, pp. 4-5.

[13] Their educational status, however, has been upgraded during recent years. In the designated neighborhood in 1940, the median years of education for persons 25 or over was 7.3 and in 1950, 8.4. This not only represents an increase within the group but also in comparison to the city medians an absolute increase in educational standing. Michael A. La Sorte, *Ecological Patterning of Farnam Courts and Its Environs*, Neighborhood Improvement Project, New Haven, Conn., unpublished paper. Tables 24 and 42.

[14] Hollingshead and Redlich, *op. cit.*, p. 126. The author's tabulation for Class V was 59 per cent.

[15] For a more comprehensive review of the sexual relationship among low-income couples as well as attitudes toward contraception, see Rainwater, *op. cit.*, pp. 92-166.

[16] Research suggestive of this proposition can be found in Leontine Young's, *Study Syndromes of Parents of Neglected and Abused Children,* unpublished doctoral thesis, Columbia University School of Social Work, June, 1963.

[17] Rather, the couples related to each other more according to what Bott calls *joint organization,* or carrying out of the same activity by each mate at different times. Elizabeth Bott, *Family and Social Network* (London: Tavistock Publications Limited, 1957), pp. 52 ff. The generality of the instrumental-expressive division is treated theoretically by Talcott Parsons and Robert F. Bales, *Family Socialization and Interaction Process* (Glencoe, Ill.: The Free Press, 1955), p. 47.

[18] Charles V. Willie. *The Structure and Composition of "Problem" and "Stable" Families in Lower Income Population* (Syracuse, N.Y.: Youth Development Center, Syracuse University, 1962, mimeographed), pp. 4-5.

CHAPTER

PERSPECTIVES FOR SOCIAL
RESEARCH AND ACTION

EXTENDING THE AREA OF
RESEARCH

In the preceding chapters we have tried to sketch a conceptual framework for assessing the social functioning of the urban multi-problem family. We have sought to give evidence of the utility of this framework by showing that it differentiates between stable and disorganized families. Finally, we have used the family's present social functioning as a point of departure for studying the correlates of stability or disorganization at the beginning of the family life cycle.

There is need for restating a point made earlier, relative to the measurement of family functioning. The approach presented here makes it possible to relate sets of individual roles and the performance of tasks to specific criteria of adequacy. Role sets and tasks were organized in terms of *areas* of functioning. Standards of adequacy were spelled out as *levels* of social functioning. The choice of areas of family functioning and levels of adequacy is influenced by the nature of both the families being studied and the social systems around them (such as the community, social class, network of agencies) with which the family interacts. Assessment of social functioning of families living in cultural settings substantially different from those surrounding the urban multi-problem family would require a modification of areas and levels of functioning.

In each instance the importance of tasks performed and criteria of adequacy established by the community would dictate the precise nature of the model for evaluation. In short, the utility of the approach to evaluation presented here rests in the tying together of concepts rather than in the use of the instrument per se. Researchers or practitioners concerned with measuring family functioning will need to examine carefully the appropriateness of the St. Paul Scale of Family Functioning for the population they wish to study. They must be ready to invest in such modifications and adaptations of the present model as the research setting may call for. That is to say, at this stage social work research has not yet produced—and is not likely to do so in the near future—evaluative instruments which can be generally applied even within one culture. Evaluation will thus have to rely on continuous efforts to create and adapt research tools to differing and changing modes of behavior, cultural expectations, and values.

Though the investment for purposes of measuring family functioning is quite considerable, the utility of the approach seems to justify this expenditure of time and effort. The method used here for evaluating family functioning provided us with a profile of the multi-problem family. Profiling rendered possible a comparison of families with various degrees of disorganization, and it also opened the door to a study of change or movement over a given time period. Lastly, the present approach provided a vantage point from which to study the development of stability or disorganization during the family life cycle.

In the present volume this latter took the form of an ex post facto study, going back from the families' present state of functioning to the beginnings of the family life cycle, in order to discover antecedents of present multi-problem behavior. The use of retrospective data imposed considerable limitations on the kind of information which could be utilized in the analysis. Reliance was placed mainly on objective, descriptive data and on information related to important events in the lives of the persons interviewed.

The rather consistent differences in various types of family functioning between stable and disorganized families early in the family life cycle leaves room for hope that early identification can become a reality. If the early partnership of the families which become disorganized tends to be characterized by conflict, poor planning, unrealistic expectations about married life, and preoccupation with self to the exclusion of others, it should be possible to develop—by means of multi-variate analysis—indices which allow a fair degree of predictability on future family functioning. Such predictability is the most important gateway to prevention or intervention before social disorganization has invaded intrafamilial, extrafamilial, and instrumental areas of family life.

The research design used in this study leaves us with major gaps in knowledge. What is the rhythm and timing of the disorganization process? Given an association between early and later malfunctioning, is disorganization a continuous, unilinear process or is it cyclical in nature marked by periodic "highs"? What is the influence of institutional factors such as housing project residence and housing authority policy upon family functioning?

The last question can be answered by means of research with populations in different types of housing, but the two previous questions can be dealt with reliably only by means of a longitudinal design. Such a study, however costly and time consuming, minimizes the research hazards inherent in responses based upon recall of events and situations several years back. It strengthens data collection through direct observation of some of the facts otherwise seen only through the eyes of the respondent.

If these concluding statements relative to the need for longitudinal studies sound too much like many a closing statement about the need for further research, it may be stated in defense that short-term, cross-sectional studies like the present one are important prerequisites to a longitudinal approach. In the absence of a body of theory on family disorganization, a long-term research venture could well become a shot in the dark. The availability of monographic findings, preferably from diverse setting, can give scope and direction to longitudinal research on multi-problem functioning.

IMPLICATIONS FOR IDENTIFYING MULTI-PROBLEM FAMILIES

Although the number of multi-problem families on which our own research data are based is less than two hundred, and even though the early identification study covers only 75 cases, we believe that the consistency in our findings and in those of the few investigators who devote themselves to this area of research makes it possible to discuss implications for action.

The first point to be made under this heading pertains to the identification of family disorganization. The Vancouver survey furnished the best evidence available so far showing the concentration of multi-problem families in low-status neighborhoods.[1] Numerous other inventories of selected groups of multi-problem families show a very high incidence of dependency on public assistance.

The connection between multi-problem behavior, as defined by us, and poverty is not far fetched. The nexus between the two phenomena is, in fact, partly conceptual. Multi-problem functioning means relative inadequacy in instrumental behavior which, by our definition, covers economic, health, and household practices. Failure in economic functioning has a direct influence upon the other two areas. Poverty, by itself, is not to be equated with inadequacy in economic practices as defined by us. Yet, poverty is the chief reason for families' failure to attain job security and manage financially. Families with adequate financial resources are in a much better position to maintain an adequate level of instrumental functioning than the economically deprived. Even though only a minor proportion of these are identified as multi-problem,[2] the vast bulk of seriously disorganized families are poor and reside in the low-income areas of the community.

These observations are pertinent to the process of identifying multi-problem families. An unspecified but large number of communities in this country and abroad have become sufficiently alarmed over the behavior of problem or multi-problem or hard-core families to institute programs of action aimed at helping these families.[3] A resolution to help requires identification of those to be helped. Few of these programs are aimed at serving the maximum number of families viewed as pathological in the community. Treatment resources are generally too limited for such an undertaking. Yet, social service systems geared to action are nearly always interested in the parameter of family pathology, if for no reason other than service planning for the future.

We attempted to show in Chapter 3 that the identification of some multi-problem families poses no great obstacles.

More than that, given a clear definition of the concept, community-wide identification can be carried out quite effectively and without great expense by means of checklist surveys of cases known to social welfare agencies. Our awareness of poverty as an almost common denominator in multi-problem family functioning, as defined here, furnishes us with a further guide to identifying these families. The process of identification need not cover the whole community but can, instead, be confined to specified target areas known for their low level of income, high unemployment, economic dependency, and, except in the case of low-cost public housing projects, deteriorated housing.

Some multi-problem functioning will undoubtedly be located outside these areas and may occasionally be found in prosperous neighborhoods. Its incidence, however, is too small to justify surveying higher status areas. Moreover, multi-problem families in middle-income neighborhoods have a way of not coming to the attention of the community, even though they exhibit nonconforming behavior.

THE LOCATION OF SERVICES TO MULTI-PROBLEM FAMILIES

Knowledge about the link between poverty and multi-problem family functioning is of crucial concern to service planning. Such knowledge determines the nature of service and where it is to be located. The ecology of family disorganization would seem to dictate the placing of services (1) in neighborhoods where the problem is prevalent, and (2) in the hands of agencies which are equipped to cope with multi-problem behavior.

The latter point is actually more complex than appears at first blush. Nearly all multi-problem families have had some contact with public assistance during their life cycle. Over half the number of such families in any urban community are likely to be known to assistance agencies at any one point in time. These facts are sometimes viewed as sufficient reason for lodging services to multi-problem families with public assistance. This argument completely disregards the more important question of whether public assistance is geared to cope with family disorganization. The 1956 Social Security Act amendments which put greater emphasis upon service to families,[4] and the more recent reorganization of the Social Security Administration leading to the placement of the public assistance function in the Bureau of Family Service, are evidence of a national trend to link assistance with appropriate services. The translation of this federal policy into local action is a slow process which advances in various communities at different rates of speed. The readiness of any given assistance agency to serve multi-problem families would hinge upon its ability to perceive the needs of disorganized families, (as contrasted with families which are merely economically dependent), to furnish trained and experienced social workers, to give diagnostic and treatment services, and to arrange case loads in such a way as to allow for intensive as well as long-term service where the need is indicated.

There may be some administrative gain in having agencies such as public assistance, protective services, and probation assume responsibility for multi-problem families. The more important condition for the placement of service responsibility rests with the agencies' readiness and capacity for rendering such service. These qualities are present in some settings; in others they may need to be cultivated through prolonged efforts by lay and professional groups. A clear distinction must be made between climate of opinion favoring a course of action and capacity based upon experience, skills, and budget to engage in an undertaking. A present nation-wide climate favors services and projects on behalf of multi-problem families. Few communities, on the other hand, have at their disposal the treatment resources or the administrative structure necessary for engaging in endeavors beyond small demonstration projects.

THE SEARCH FOR FACTORS UNDERLYING FAMILY DISORGANIZATION

The recognition that multi-problem families are predominantly poor families spotlights poverty as *a* causal agent in family disorganization. Poverty provides the breeding ground for multi-problem behavior as it does for crime and juvenile delinquency, although poverty is not a sufficient cause for these and other types of deviant behavior. The factors or combination of factors that lead to family disorganization are far from clear at this stage. The data reported in Chapter 5 suggest the presence of certain relationship patterns and values early in the family life cycle which predispose the family toward social disorganization. This led to a hypothesis, which could not be tested by the data of the present research, postulating personality defects as an underlying force in problem behavior. Our data, on the other hand, provided no evidence that such defects, if they do exist, take on the dimension of psychoses or serious character disorders. Their incidence, judging from this and an earlier study,[5] is too small to explain family malfunctioning in most of the families. Our own data indicate that 16 per cent of the treatment group and 5 per cent of the comparison (more stable) families had a history of diagnosed mental illness. Since the interviewers had no access to agency records but relied on self-reports in families in the comparison group, the extent of mental illness among these families is probably understated.

Evidence regarding behavior differences is provided by our analysis of factors which differentiate between stable and disorganized families (Table 6). Among the five factors discriminating most sharply between these groups of families are the behavior of the father (rank no. 1) and the behavior of the mother (rank no. 5). Individual Behavior and Adjustment of the parents, it will be recalled, denotes the manner in which family heads perform their socially expected roles and get along with the world around them. Failure in this area is not composed of any one form of defect or deviancy but ranges from the absence of necessary social skills (such as the ability to act confidently when applying for a job) to outright delinquent behavior. The personality factors underlying these modes of behavior are not known. Their most common denominator, in terms of our level of analysis, is nonconformity or inability to act according to social expectation. This is particularly true for behavior that comprehends marital relationships, child care, and the maintenance of family solidarity. These together with the behavior of the father and mother are the five most salient factors which set off stable from disorganized families.

Nonconformity thus pertains chiefly to family relationship roles. Other family roles of an instrumental nature, such as health practices, physical care of children, and money management, also differentiate between stable and multi-problem families. The way some community resources such as health and social agencies are used serves as a partial index of family disorganization. Use of church, by contrast, is a factor with almost no discriminatory power. Source and amount of income, the nature of the job, informal social activities, and the physical condition of the home do not clearly separate problem families from nonproblem families.

The nonconformity of disorganized families, it appears, encompasses mainly behavior requiring interpersonal competence in dealing with members of the family. Behavior toward relatives, friends, agencies, school, and church is more conforming, at least by comparison with standards shown by stable lower-class families.

This observation has a bearing upon the often voiced comment that multi-problem families are lower-class families whose distinguishing characteristic is cultural nonconformity. This is tantamount to defining the multi-problem population as a subculture. Such a definition is useful only to the extent that we are able to show that multi-problem families share attributes of behavior and values which are different from the population surrounding them. Our research is too narrow in scope clearly to affirm or deny this contention. It is particularly on the value dimension that our data are limited. On the other hand, our research does show that multi-problem families share many of the attributes and behaviors of other lower-class families (see Chapter 4) while differing sharply in a few respects from the latter. Hence, the designation lower-class nonconforming behavior does not represent an adequate definition of multi-problem functioning.

Regardless of whether or not the term subculture is applicable to multi-problem families, their shared characteristic of an inability to perform familial roles adequately becomes a focus for diagnosis and treatment. Diagnostic data require detailed descriptive information on present functioning, psychometric measurements which can be related to behavioral norms, and developmental histories on families and individuals. The importance of the latter was highlighted by our own background data on disorganized families. Our findings would seem to indicate that multi-problem functioning has roots in the past, which can be traced, first, to the beginning of the family life cycle and, second, to the parents' family of orientation. The latter thesis received additional support in an unpublished Rutgers master's thesis in which a correlation of +.56 (Gamma) was found between functioning of families of orientation and procreation.[6]

This continuity in problem behavior from one generation to the next suggests the presence of attributes which permeate home life in general and the socialization of children in particular. What these attributes may be, can be learned only from longitudinal research. From our knowledge of problem families we are able to suggest some multi-problem characteristics which may be transmitted through the socialization process, in the nature of failings or deficiencies denoting the absence rather than the presence of traits. They include lack of communication skills, lack of ability to form close relationships, the absence of self-confidence and trust in others,[7] an inability to give but a dominating wish to receive, a strong need for immediate gratification, and a commensurate inability to postpone it. All these are reflected to varying degrees in the present functioning and the background histories of the families studied, and are also the characteristics which social workers have come to know. Their very nature lends support to the thesis of Harriet Wilson, which states that multi-problem families should be viewed "not as a manifestation of a specific subculture, but as an index of the breakdown of a culture."[8]

If data in Chapters 3 and 4 have helped us to pinpoint those areas of functioning in which multi-problem families are least adequate, our analysis can supply us at best with a hypothesis on etiology. The array of profile categories, based on scalogramming of 150 disorganized families, would seem to suggest that family disorganization proceeds from the intrafamilial relationship area to relationships beyond the family proper, and then to functioning of a more instrumental nature (see Figure 1 in Chapter 3 and the text immediately following it). Families which barely manage to maintain the family as a physical unit are usually beset by serious problems in their social relationships. The reverse is seldom true.

If longitudinal analysis should verify that the flow of family disorganization moves in the direction postulated above, the question of causation would still not have received a decisive answer. It is not far-fetched to assume that problem behavior in relationships and in instrumental functioning is affected by a common underlying factor. Poverty, which in our society implies social as well as economic deprivation, may be such a factor. Poverty, though it is not a sufficient condition, may be a necessary or nearly necessary condition for bringing about a situation in which families become vulnerable to the point where the social, emotional, and physical welfare of members are threatened, and family unity reaches a low ebb or vanishes all together.

The fact that the majority of economically deprived families remain socially stable is a theoretically interesting phenomenon, but it provides no justification for the existence of poverty in America. This country has a moral responsibility to eliminate poverty because it is the most formidable handicap to the fulfillment of the American credo, equality of opportunity for all. The eradication of poverty would also remove the most clearly identified seedbed on which delinquency, neglect, ill health, and various forms of social disorganization, including multi-problem family functioning, are known to flourish.

IMPLICATIONS FOR SERVICE TO MULTI-PROBLEM FAMILIES

At this stage the patient reader may well ask whether the gaps in knowledge which we sought to expose here fully will not prevent us from drawing implications for services to multi-problem families. The answer can be given only in relation to the goals and values of social work which carry a commitment to serve wherever the need for service exists. The social work profession aims at having service rest upon a scientific base—that is, a storehouse of organized knowledge which permits the formulation and testing of theories. The backbone of scientific social work is verified knowledge about the effects of intervention by practitioners in situations of unmet need.

Social work is only at the beginning of the road leading to the goal enunciated above. Yet, the need to render service is ever present, regardless of the strength of the scientific base at a particular point in time. Gaps in knowledge confronting practice exist in many areas and are not unique to the field of multi-problem family treatment. A study like our own presents some beginning information which, together with other research findings accumulating in the field, enables us to go a step beyond offering enlightened guesses to the field. It is in this vein that our comments on implications for practice should be viewed.

In Chapter 1 we cited evidence from a survey done by Lagey and Ayres that at least 143 communities with a population of 100,000 and over [9] in the United States and Canada are engaged in some kind of effort aimed at dealing with the problems of the multi-problem family. On the basis of information supplied by the services or projects in the survey, Lagey and Ayres were able to arrive at the following classification of approaches which are quoted here by percentage frequency:

Intensive casework approach (37.3%)

Case conference approach (20.3%)

Multiservice approach (16.9%)

Community development approach (13.6%)

Other approaches, comprising a variety of services such as volunteer case aide programs, home maker projects, and special information and referral services (3.4%).

A residual category, "could not be classified" (8.5%), was established by the researchers for communities from which no material was received by the time of report publication.[10]

For a full definition of these approaches and a description

of services and projects, the reader is referred to the excellent survey monograph by Lagey and Ayres.[11] We shall briefly summarize the Lagey and Ayres definitions and comment on the four major approaches in the light of findings from our own study.

Intensive Casework Approach

It is no accident that casework treatment is the most frequently used approach in service to multi-problem families. The early history of professional social work in America revolves around casework, and at present the vast majority of students in schools of social work select casework as their primary method. Most social work positions are classified as casework or its equivalent, and to persons motivated to embark upon a social work career the one-to-one relationship appears to symbolize most clearly the idea of the helping profession. The psychiatric tradition with its emphasis on intervention by a single therapist continues to be strong in social work.

The extensive use of casework in programs designed to help the multi-problem family is in no small measure due to the prevalence of psychiatric thinking and theory in social work. Traditional psychiatry, in contrast to social psychiatry which is slowly gaining ground, is mainly concerned with individual deviancy and problems of personality and relationships. Although social work rather than psychiatry took the initiative in developing methods and services for helping the multi-problem family, psychiatric theory and method were nonetheless influential in defining the role of the casework practitioner in this area.

Two considerations go into a decision to extend intensive services to multi-problem families: first, that most of these families have not been receiving casework or have been served only sporadically; and, second, that the traditional casework approach, predicated upon a client who shows some motivation for accepting treatment, needs to be modified. The latter point has given rise to modifications of the more conventional casework techniques. These changes include reaching out to the hard-to-reach or resistive by using a direct and if necessary assertive approach allied with home visiting; focusing on the diagnosis and treatment of the whole family rather than individual members only; frequently visiting the family, possible because of reduced worker case load; and co-ordinating diverse services by using one social worker for the family unit.

The primary treatment goal is the improvement of social functioning, particularly relationships among family members and in contacts with the community. Lesser emphasis in treatment is placed upon insight therapy or personality reorganization.

This modified casework approach to multi-problem families, sometimes referred to as family centered treatment, has been very well described in the *Casework Notebook* by Overton and Tinker.[12] Of all the service approaches to multi-problem families, the intensive casework approach is discussed most widely in the social work literature. Articles and books on the subject tend to be descriptive rather than analytical and are mainly concerned with setting forth method and relating case material; systematic research is relatively scarce.[13]

The intensive casework approach is predicated upon a view of the multi-problem family as composed of people who have lost hope, feel rejected by society, and have limited their contacts to the bare minimum necessary for physical survival. Casework is seen as the basic tool which can re-establish communication and modify the family's attitudes toward society by demonstrating tangible support and partnership in working out problems besetting the family.

The Profile of Family Functioning presented in earlier

chapters supports this view of the multi-problem family. Family relations are defective, and family contacts with the community are problematic. Social activities are restricted and generally devoid of opportunities for fun and relaxation; and family members do not make use of community resources except when forced by a serious crisis or emergency to seek outside help.

Casework is the outstretched hand of society, symbolizing hope and trust in a process of joint problem solving. This process, however, is likely to begin with tangible difficulties which the family can easily perceive: community resources required for meeting various needs are drawn in; and then, after a worker-client relationship has been established, there is concentration on the family's interpersonal problems. There is no doubt that this extended hand is an important symbolic gesture, but it raises three inevitable questions: How representative is this hand? How powerful is it? Is the family ready to grasp it?

The last point is partially answered by the experience of many projects in serving disorganized families. Establishing a treatment relationship is a slow process, extending over weeks and sometimes months. The modal period of service is between 24 and 30 months. Once accepted, however, few cases can manage without welfare services thereafter,[14] and service on an attenuated basis needs to be continued by some agency or agencies. The outstretched hand is grasped but slowly. It is held loosely or firmly, but rarely abandoned entirely.

How representative is the outstretched hand? This is an important question, for it asks whether that hand is a lone hand or is given in the name of the community. Are other agencies a part of the team, are they ready to join a family community partnership, or will they continue to operate in an atmosphere of mutual distrust? The structure of projects bringing service to multi-problem families has much to do with the way these questions are answered. If other agencies and service systems, such as assistance, health, education, and corrections, do not move in step with the worker rendering casework services, his lone hand may soon lose its grasp.

The relative power of the outstretched hand is a most crucial issue. Family centered casework is focused, particularly in its beginning stages, upon visible, concrete need, bound up with economic deprivation, limited opportunities for jobs, and slum living.

Intensive casework, as it views the multiple needs of the client family, seeks to strengthen those traits among family members which enable them to take fuller advantage of existing opportunities in work, education, health care, recreation, and so on. Such casework efforts, however, are circumscribed by the opportunities provided by the community. The opportunity structures, to use Merton's term,[15] represent the precise limits within which the social worker can help his client to improve his functioning. The worker, most likely representing one social agency in the community, has only limited power to modify the opportunity structure. The caseworker's most effective intervention may serve to give to members of disorganized families an unbiased interpretation of the role of agencies; and to social agencies, the worker may supply an insightful account of the problems of the multi-problem families. This activity should lead to improved ways of meeting client needs in many areas, including economic assistance and health. There is some evidence that this is the case.[16]

Such activities, important as they undoubtedly are, make only a small dent in the over-all opportunity structure. They do not, for instance, provide an income which permits a mode of living above the poverty line; they do not enable the major wage earner to land a secure and well-paying job; they do not remove the children from neighborhoods where they are strongly exposed to juvenile delinquency.

Intensive casework, which generally represents the liberal conscience of society, thus acts with the approval but not with the support of society. For that reason various programs and projects, using intensive casework as a primary method, have sought to involve broader sectors of society by operating as an alliance of agencies, or as a new service on whose lay board and advisory committee members of existing agencies and institutions are represented. Furthermore, the intensive casework approach tends to be coupled with efforts at community-wide education in the problems of the disorganized families and in the ways designed to further their rehabilitation.

How effective is the intensive casework approach in its objective of family rehabilitation? This approach, as well as the other above-mentioned approaches, is employed without the benefit of precise knowledge regarding its effectiveness. The few existing projects, set up to evaluate the effect of service with the aid of control groups, are still in process. Most casework programs for treating multi-problem families operate without adequate instruments of evaluation.

Research evidence has accumulated in the social work literature which shows that the rendering of social casework service as part of an assistance program results in significantly more client change or movement than the receipt of assistance without service. One of the best-designed studies in support of this hypothesis, carried out by John Behling, found that casework services utilizing small case loads were also somewhat more effective in helping multi-problem families than those with large case loads.[17] The St. Paul movement study of 150 families and the two-year follow-up of 51 cases found movement in two or three areas of functioning during treatment and continued improvement after closing.[18] No control groups were available to assess the relative influence of treatment as compared to other factors which may have produced movement.

Although conclusive proof about the value of intensive casework is not yet available, the converging evidence points to its being responsible for some modifications in client behavior. The typical movement pattern for each family, as stated elsewhere, is not one of drastic improvement but rather one of small gains in a few areas of social functioning.[19] These gains seemingly endure beyond the termination of intensive services, but continued service from one or more agencies is generally necessary. Casework services are helpful in changing the client's disposition of estrangement, apathy, resentment, and often hostility toward the world around him, to one of greater dependence upon social agencies. Generally the families' biggest gain in treatment is in learning to ask for help, and yet the kind of assistance they need is not really viewed with favor by the larger community. To supply an interpretation of the families' dependent status more favorable than that held by the community (public opinion, advertisement, press, and other news media) is one of the main functions of intensive casework.

Yet casework, operating in the name of one or more well-meaning welfare services, is not in a position to alter the physical and social environment in which multi-problem families are living. Social welfare in this country operates in fact with a very limited mandate: to help the socially handicapped. It is not charged with removing the conditions which give rise to social handicaps. Intensive casework aims largely at coping with inadequacies inherent in the multi-problem family.

Such inadequacies, whatever their cause, are real. But they are feeding on a situation which can serve only to perpetuate them. Casework by itself, no matter how intensive, provides at best a shield against a system which does not open its arms to the lower-class, multi-problem family. Occasionally casework treatment enables a family to take the big step out of the multi-problem orbit into more stable society,[20] but for most families, social work helps to make available to them a new frame of reference for problem solving and a basis of support in the midst of a problem ridden existence.

Social workers serving multi-problem families observe correctly that most of these families are in need of continued support until the children leave home. The explanation sometimes advanced cites personal immaturity and extensive character disorders as reasons for the need for continued support. The preponderance of character disorders in disorganized families has not been demonstrated. Immaturity, however, may be interpreted to mean unreadiness or inability to assume the responsibilities of stable family living. The profiles of the multi-problem families in the present volume support this view.

If deficiencies in values and behavior can be traced to poor home background, deprived living, and restricted opportunities, how much change may we expect as a result of personal intervention which leaves the over-all social structure basically unchanged? The sparse research evidence available points to limited gains particularly in those areas where the casework effort has been most concentrated.[21] Little gain was noted in areas such as health and economic functioning where social work was relatively powerless to improve the families' position. This observation, which needs further substantiation, can serve as a vantage point for critically examining the role of intensive casework in the service to multi-problem families.

The Case Conference Approach

The case conference approach, the second in frequency according to the Lagey-Ayres survey, carries a limited commitment to action but gives recognition to the fact that the multi-problem family is the responsibility of many social agencies. This approach is often a first step taken by communities who wish to develop better services to the multi-problem family.[22] The case conference method acknowledges the need for community-wide co-ordination of the many services directed to the multi-problem family.

Lagey and Ayres define the approach as involving "a presentation of material about a case from various members of a formally assembled group, formulation of a group diagnosis and treatment plan, and assignment of responsibility for treatment (or parts of a treatment plan) to an agency or agencies. It may include a follow-up of cases through periodic review, and assessment of results." [23]

The writers point out further that public as well as private welfare agencies join in case conferences, usually under the auspices of one organization. In communities where a welfare council or council of agencies is operating, that body is likely to sponsor the case conferences. Though such conferences represent most often a meeting of social workers from such diverse fields as public welfare, family service, child guidance, corrections, education, and health; the meetings may also bring together additional professional disciplines such as psychiatry, clinical psychology, and medicine.[24]

The case conference approach takes into account not only the multiplicity of problems affecting the family but also the many services and professional skills which need to be involved in dealing with these problems. The case conference represents a first effort at getting together. It lays the groundwork for a common approach, and supplies concrete instances or cases which illustrate the need for a joint effort.

Case conferences have considerable diagnostic value since they provide a more complete and more balanced picture of each family than is contained in the information available to each agency. In that sense and also because joint acknowledgment of a problem situation constitutes motivation toward action, the case conference undoubtedly serves to strengthen treatment services. It does little, however, to modify the nature of treatment. The case conference allocates treatment to the various specialists, those agencies which have been doing it all along. No new patterns of accountability or methods of co-ordinating or performing treatment are established by this process. From an administrative viewpoint, case conferences are a luxury that few agencies can afford except on a demonstration basis or as an educational device in staff training. The conferences make a heavy demand on professional and clerical staff time, the latter being devoted to arranging meetings and preparing typed records. Even if each meeting scheduled deals with several cases, the question must still be posed whether the results justify the investment.

The case conference, in short, is chiefly an educational device which can help agencies to become attuned to the problem and practitioners to become more knowledgeable in diagnosis and community resources. As a device for serving the multi-problem family, the case conference approach is inefficient, unwieldy, and too limited in its objective to be recommended. In an ongoing operation devoted to helping the disorganized family, the function of the case conference can be taken over by a screening and treatment planning committee which at one and the same time attends to the selection of families, case assignment, and continuous planning and co-ordination of the over-all treatment process.

The Multi-Service Approach

This approach, in contrast to the case conference, acknowledges the need for a commitment to service from the various agencies whose knowledge and skill can contribute to the welfare of the multi-problem family. However, a more basic consideration here is the theoretical notion that diag-

nosis and treatment of problem behavior must address itself
to the various social systems in which members of disorganized families play a role. The multi-service approach con-
cedes the importance of the family in shaping and influencing the behavior of its members. At the same time the
approach notes the parallel influences, at times outweighing
those of the home, of neighborhood, school system, peer
groups, and the like, upon the personality of the family
members and upon the functioning of the family group. The
multi-service approach is in line with our empirical findings,
showing a close correlation between social functioning in
roles within the home (such as family relationships and
child care) and outside the home (school, work, and social
activities).[25] This approach postulates, therefore, that service to families can be made more effective when it encompasses the multiple roles in which family members are
usually involved.

Lagey and Ayres, on the basis of their survey, observe
that a co-ordinated or integrated treatment plan, using various combinations of casework, group work, and community
organization, forms the core of the multi-service approach. It
is often carried out on an area or neighborhood basis, and
activities are co-ordinated through periodic meetings of the
various agencies involved. The administrative structure of
the multi-service approach may vary considerably. Frequently primary responsibility for administering or co-ordinating the program rests with a neighborhood center or
settlement house. A public housing authority, a health and
welfare council, a public welfare district office, or a combination of social agencies may co-ordinate the services of
the program; at other times a separate organization is established for purposes of service co-ordination. A wide
variety of services may be offered to various age groups,
ranging from preschool nurseries to senior citizens' clubs.[26]

Improving the neighborhood as a whole is a basic consideration in the multi-service approach. Its aim is to render a diversity of services which will help families directly and contribute to a more favorable image of neighborhood and community. The underlying assumption of the neighborhood based multi-service approach holds that an improvement in the neighborhood image will lead residents to acquire a more positive identification with the neighborhood and enable them to play a more constructive role in their daily contacts.[27]

Since the multi-service approach may involve help in a great many areas, an infinite variety of service patterns is found. The emphasis tends to differ not only in keeping with the needs of the client population but also in accordance with the types of agency present, their willingness to serve, their influence in the community and the quality of their services. The larger the number of agencies participating, the more formidable the task of co-ordinating the over-all program.

The multi-service approach may include intensive casework services to multi-problem families, and other services including casework may be available to the total neighborhood in which the problem families reside. Although the program may encompass a great many services to individuals and groups, the emphasis in this approach is upon meeting needs through the use of health, welfare, recreational, and group work services. No research data on the effectiveness of this approach are yet available. The complexity of the service pattern, the large number of people affected, and the difficulty of controlling the effects of services given, constitute major obstacles to rigorous, evaluative research in this area.

The Community Development Approach

In the community development approach the multi-problem family is viewed as one manifestation of the many types of social disorganization which prevail in urban centers of the United States. Community development programs serve multi-problem families as one segment of a lower-class, socially and economically deprived population. Theoretically the community development approach, like the multi-service one, holds that the disorganized family is part of the larger community and can be helped effectively only by treating it within the context of its roles in relation to the surrounding community. Unlike the multi-service approach, community development calls for massive intervention in areas of social disorganization, the so-called gray areas of the city. It uses such means as creating employment opportunities, providing vocational training and retraining, improving housing, bettering educational opportunities, giving more adequate medical and public health services, planning comprehensive recreational facilities, and making available better welfare services. Political action and the use of indigenous leaders—by means of leadership training programs—are two ways of involving the local population in the total program.[28]

The community development approach seeks to work through existing community agencies and organizations including schools, neighborhood centers, ethnic associations, and churches, to the extent that any or all of these can be involved. On the other hand, the program may establish as many new services as are required to meet existing need. The over-all responsibility for planning, co-ordinating and rendering services usually rests with either a specially created body operating under a mandate of the city council, community health and welfare council, department of welfare, housing authority, or with a group of organizations joined together for the express purpose of planning such a program. Extensive financial support from outside sources, usually foundations or federal grant-giving agencies, appears to be the rule.

Community development programs are frequently a synthesis of physical and social urban renewal. They were given impetus by the discovery that physical renewal in the form of low-income housing developments results in limited gains only, largely in living space, physical health, conditions of the furnishings, and social participation in the neighborhood.[29] New housing per se, it has been observed, has little positive effect on the over-all social situation of a resettled population.[30] Quite the contrary, police statistics on crime and delinquency tend to pinpoint public housing projects as centers of deviant behavior. Community development programs variously referred to as human renewal, neighborhood development, opening opportunities, have become the social counterparts to the physical program of urban redevelopment. Although physical and social renewal are intimately related, the two programs seldom work under the same auspices. The characteristic pattern leaves community development with the task of helping people adjust to the situation left in the wake of physical renewal. But at least two of the projects listed in the Lagey-Ayres survey included preoccupancy planning in public housing. There are also early signs that the social situation depicted by Jane Jacobs and others [31] is having an effect upon the planning of urban housing.

The community development approach to human deprivation in general and the multi-problem family in particular attempts to bring about the kind of far-reaching environmental changes which will directly affect the opportunity structure. The changed environment is seen to provide a more fertile soil than the old environment for those who are socially and psychologically handicapped.

The ideal objective in the community development approach—the substantial modification of the environment of the deprived population—is an exceedingly big order. Such modification is more typically the product of social revolutions. In actuality, the community development programs listed in the survey are carried out on a more modest scale. The emphasis tends to be on youth and centers around education, employment, and recreation. Services to total families, work with aged, health care, housing, et cetera, are given differential stress in different projects. The community development approach is clearly global and macroscopic in nature. Implicit in this approach is the notion that the social functioning of such severely deprived groups as the multi-problem family will be considerably improved.

The community development programs listed in the Lagey-Ayres survey are of very recent origin. None of them has reached the stage where research evaluation is possible. The problems of evaluation listed under the multi-service approach exist here but in magnified form. The strength of these programs is largely a theoretical one, for they conceive of multi-problem functioning not as an isolated phenomenon but as the product of the total social situation. Treatment, accordingly, is not narrowed to a limited number of services, but it comprehensively employs the major economic, health, welfare, and education systems in the community. That this kind of total program has not yet seen the light of day is no reflection on the soundness of the idea.

MULTI-PROBLEM FAMILIES OR MULTI-PROBLEM WELFARE SYSTEM

The intensive casework approach and the community development approach to treating the multi-problem family represent different emphases in dealing with the problem. The former concentrates attention upon the family itself and endeavors to help it adjust to the environment. The latter focuses upon the environment and seeks to modify it in a way which will aid deprived populations including the multi-problem families.

The casework method does not preclude the use of specific techniques designed to bring about changes in the environment; nor does the community development approach exclude measures especially aimed at helping the disorganized family. The difference is mainly one of emphasis. But beyond that, divergent philosophies characterize the two approaches. The starting point of intensive casework is the all-pervasive concern with family disorganization. Community development, as used in this chapter, has its origin in the view that the existing social conditions, which include the nature of the welfare services, set severe limits on efforts to improve the lot of the socially handicapped individual or family. Accordingly, social action is focused more narrowly upon the problem families and the agencies concerned with them, or more broadly upon those social conditions which are seen as having given rise to and perpetuated multi-problem functioning. The selection of the casework approach in coping with family disorganization, though not implying the acceptance of the environmental status quo, does signify a choice of highest priority for working directly with the socially most handicapped in society. The hoped-for goal in this approach is the elevation of the deprived to a level of functioning more nearly in line with societal expectations. The philosophy of community development, though not denying the deviant character of the multi-problem families, holds that broad societal adjustments would in themselves bring about the accommodation of the socially handicapped. One of the risks inherent in this global approach resides in the possibility that the multi-problem family, because of its socially marginal character, may not benefit or may least benefit from broad social reform.

The concept multi-problem family puts the spotlight on the family and evaluates functioning in terms of given community norms regarding values and behavior. In the absence of such norms, functioning could not possibly be judged as adequate or inadequate. Moreover, the use of the concept makes an implicit assumption that multi-problem functioning is not likely to be a modal response among the many families in a given area. Although very few environments seem to create more disorganized than stable families, the assumption above must not be taken to imply independence between family functioning and social environment.

The social work literature provides countless illustrations of the segmental nature of and lack of co-ordination among social services. This state of affairs hits the multi-problem family with its many needs particularly hard. This family, already suspicious and distrustful, becomes thoroughly confused and intractable when confronted with elaborate statutes of eligibility and complex and overlapping lines of authority. Although the multi-problem family is characteristically crisis oriented—that is, it asks for help only when there is a severe threat to the well-being of family members —it should also be remembered that many social welfare systems are responsive only to the crisis approach. Inadequate financial provisions, lack of needed services, or long waiting lists in existing services are but a few manifestations of a community's limited responsiveness to multi-problem need.

A family's failure to avail itself of required help may well be the result of the community's failure to respond properly to a call for aid or even its insensitivity to need. The single most important aspect of the intensive, family centered casework approach is the appointment of a practitioner who "sensitizes" himself and the community to family need and helps create conditions for helful intervention. The absence of community agents and agencies able to perceive and respond to multiple need may thus constitute a multi-problem condition inherent in the social welfare system.

The functioning of families and that of social agencies, we believe, are reciprocally related. The existence of multi-problem families brings about the presence of a service pattern which can respond to their needs. As services become sensitized to the requirements of multi-problem families and institute methods of meeting these needs, multi-problem functioning becomes accessible and amenable to treatment. The severity of family malfunctioning as defined by concepts selected in this book is at least partly a function of the availability of appropriate services. Problematic family functioning and inadequate agency functioning may be viewed as two sides of the same coin.

The selection of the most appropriate service focus remains a question that each community must decide for itself. The multiple service approach furnishes the minimum conditions for filling in gaps in services, co-ordinating existing agency activities, and approaching the family, not as a conglomeration of unrelated needs, but as an organic unit which must be treated within the context of services to the neighborhood and community. The community development approach, as stated earlier, is global; for it constitutes, in a way, a tacit acknowledgment of the fact that more than welfare services are involved in helping the multi-problem family. Community development tends to overlook however, the very special problems presented by severe family disorganization. Insufficient heed is paid to the long-standing pattern, often transmitted over generations, of economic dependency and persistent failure to cope with the day-by-day problems of life. The community development approach aims high, looks for basic causes, and works toward prevention, but frequently loses sight of those families already severely damaged and frantically engaged in the struggle with life.

The intensive casework approach, though perhaps it is not fully attuned to the numerous factors which produce and perpetuate the multi-problem family, does concentrate firmly and persistently upon the fate of the multi-problem family. In keeping with the tradition of social casework this approach endeavors to help the families attain a level of adjustment and interpersonal competence at which they can function independently. Though this goal is often beyond reach, intensive casework establishes full and continued responsibility for the fate of the multi-problem family. The effectiveness of casework, like that of all other helping professions, depends to no small extent upon the skill of the worker. But casework skill is not enough, for the socially disorganized family has diverse needs which require considerable economic aid and a variety of specialized resources.

The extent to which the personal intervention of the social worker is backed up by the resources of the community is a most crucial issue in the use of intensive casework services. The social worker's role as mediator between family and community provides the bridge which can reduce the degree of alienation between the two. But the success of the worker's effort hinges largely upon the way in which the community becomes a partner to treatment by providing the means and the services needed by the multi-problem family. Effective casework service becomes at this point part of a community-wide effort. Political, social, and economic considerations will dictate the scope of this effort. As a minimum condition for attaining the goals of treatment, the multi-problem family itself must be enabled to feel that its rehabilitation is the community's compelling concern.

NOTES FOR CHAPTER 6

[1] Beverly Ayres and Joseph C. Lagey, *Checklist Survey of Multi-Problem Families in Vancouver City* (Vancouver, B.C.: Community Chest and Councils of the Greater Vancouver Area, 1961, mimeographed), pp. 34-40.

[2] Studies in New Haven, Syracuse, and Vancouver cited earlier indicate that between six and twelve per cent of families in low-income neighborhoods are seriously disorganized.

[3] For evidence see Benjamin Schlesinger, *The Multi-Problem Family: A Review and Annotated Bibliography* (Toronto: University of Toronto Press, 1963).

[4] The 1956 amendments emphasize more federal support for services intended "to promote the well-being of the Nation by encouraging the States to place greater emphasis on helping to strengthen family life and helping needy families and individuals attain the maximum economic and personal independence of which they are capable." Social Security Amendments of 1956, Public Law 880, Title III, Sec. 300, 84th Congress, second Session.

[5] Various studies on multi-problem families use diverse categories for reporting the incidence of psychosis and character disorders among parents. Sometimes, suspected and diagnosed disorders are grouped together; at other times, mental illness and deficiency are reported under one heading. Data on mental illness in families usually are not reported as unduplicated counts. As far as can be judged on the basis of unsystematic reporting fewer than one of five disorganized families are headed by psychotic or character disordered parents.

[6] The study contained a random sample of 44 young Newark families. See Walda Ciafone, Florence Bernstein, *et al., Relationship of Family Functioning to Anomie, Social Class and Other Related Factors* (New Brunswick, N.J.: Graduate School of Social Work, Rutgers, The State University, June, 1963, unpublished M.S.W. Thesis), pp. 66-77.

[7] A correlation of +.54 was found between family malfunctioning and anomie or a feeling of alienation from society. *Ibid.,* p. 43.

[8] Harriet Wilson, *Delinquency and Child Neglect* (London: George Allen and Unwin Ltd., 1962), p. 208.

[9] Smaller communities were included in the survey where a state or province had no city of 100,000 or larger. See Joseph C. Lagey, and Beverley Ayres, *Community Treatment Programs for Multi-Problem Families* (Vancouver: Community Chest and Councils of the Greater Vancouver Area, 1962), p. 5.

[10] Lagey and Ayres, *op. cit.,* p. 8, p. 149—see also Joseph C. Lagey and Beverly Ayres, "Community Treatment Programs for Multi-Problem Families," in Benjamin Schlesinger, *op. cit.,* pp. 55-71.

[11] Lagey and Ayres, *op cit.*

[12] Alice Overton and Katherine Tinker, *Casework Notebook* (St. Paul, Minn.: Family Centered Project, Greater St. Paul Community Chest and Councils, Inc., 1959).

[13] For bibliographic references see Benjamin Schlesinger, *op. cit.,* pp. 73-159.

[14] For data on services to multi-problem families two years after clos-

ing see L. L. Geismar and Beverly Ayres, *Patterns of Change in Problem Families* (St. Paul, Minn.: Family Centered Project, 1959), p. 19.

[15] Robert K. Merton, "Social Conformity, Deviation, and Opportunity Structures: A Comment on the Contributions of Dubin and Cloward," *American Sociological Review,* Vol. 24, No. 2, April, 1959, pp. 177-189.

[16] The evidence is based upon rising expenditures for families newly accepted for family centered services. The expenditures cover the main assistance for food, lodging, and health services. See Beverly Ayres, *Study of Public Assistance Costs in Family Centered Project Families from 1953 to 1958* (St. Paul, Minn.: Greater St. Paul Community Chest and Councils, Inc., Feb., 1959, mimeographed), pp. 18 ff. See also John H. Behling, *An Experimental Study to Measure the Effectiveness of Case-work Services* (Columbus, Ohio: Franklin County Welfare Department 1961; mimeographed Ph.D. dissertation, Ohio State University, 1961), p. 65.

[17] John Behling, *op. cit.,* pp. 56-62.

[18] L. L. Geismar and Beverly Ayres, *Patterns of Change in Problem Families* (St. Paul, Minn.: Family Centered Project, 1959), pp. 6-20.

[19] *Ibid.,* p. 10.

[20] Thus about 12 per cent of the families in the St. Paul study showed decided movement in nearly every area of family functioning. Only 20 per cent of the families served had contact with fewer than two agencies after completion of intensive services, *Ibid.,* p. 8 and p. 20.

[21] *Ibid.,* p. 26.

[22] Lagey and Ayres, *op. cit.,* p. 10.

[23] *Ibid.,* p. 9.

[24] *Ibid.,* p. 9.

[25] L. L. Geismar and Beverly Ayres, *Families in Trouble* (St. Paul, Minn.: Family Centered Project, 1958), p. 133.

[26] Lagey and Ayres, *op. cit.,* pp. 95-123.

[27] Ludwig L. Geismar, "Three Levels of Treatment for the Multi-Problem Family," *Social Casework,* Vol. 42, No. 3, March, 1961, pp. 124-127.

[28] Lagey and Ayres, *op. cit.,* p. 124.

[29] F. Stuart Chapin, "The Social Effects of Public Housing," in F. Stuart Chapin, *Experimental Designs in Sociological Research* (New York: Harper & Brothers, 1947). Also, Daniel Wilner, *The Housing Environment and Family Life* (Baltimore: Johns Hopkins Press, 1962). It should be noted that the studies cited and others done in this country and England cover relatively short-time periods and register the early response of residents to new structure and facilities. The early Housing Authority records of Farnam Courts, New Haven, reveal good care of public property (benches, lawn, bushes, washing machines, et cetera), much neighborliness, extensive communal activities including an active tenants' council, and other evidence of pride in the neighborhood. Fifteen years later, at the beginning of the Neighborhood Improvement Project, physical neglect of the area and apathy toward communal undertakings were striking characteristics of the housing project.

[30] Jane Jacobs, *The Death and Life of Great American Cities* (New York: Random House, Inc., 1961).

[31] *Ibid.* Also, Herbert J. Gans, *The Urban Villagers, Group and Class in the Life of Italian-Americans* (Glencoe, Ill.: The Free Press, 1962).

APPENDIX

LEVELS OF SOCIAL FUNCTIONING *

General Criteria for Levels of Social Functioning

INADEQUATE	MARGINAL	ADEQUATE
Community Has a Right to Intervene	*Behavior Not Sufficiently Harmful to Justify Intervention*	*Behavior Is in Line With Community Expectations*
Laws and/or mores are clearly violated. Behavior of family members a threat to the community.	No violation of major laws although behavior of family members is contrary to what is acceptable for status group.	Laws are obeyed and mores observed. Behavior acceptable to status group.
Family life is characterized by extreme conflict, neglect, severe deprivation, or very poor relationships resulting in physical and/or emotional suffering of family members; disruption of family life	Family life marked by conflict, apathy, or unstable relationships which are a potential threat to welfare of family members and/or the community; each crisis poses the danger of family's dis-	Family life is stable, members have a sense of belonging, family is able to handle problems without facing disruption, children are being raised in an atmosphere conducive to healthy physical and

* Reproduced with permission of the publisher from L. L. Geismar and Beverly Ayres, *Measuring Family Functioning* (St. Paul, Minn.: Family Centered Project, Greater St. Paul Community Chest and Councils, Inc., 1960), pp. 91-100. Some revisions have been made by the Neighborhood Improvement Project, New Haven, Connecticut.

INADEQUATE	MARGINAL	ADEQUATE
imminent, children in clear and present danger because of conditions above or other behavior inimical to their welfare.	ruption, but children are not in imminent danger.	emotional development. Socialization process carried out affirmatively; adequate training in social skills.

A. Family Relationships and Family Unity

1. Marital Relationship

Marital Relationship *should be checked* where either or both of the following are applicable: (1) one partner has a legal responsibility toward the other and has some contact with the family; (2) there is a continuing extramarital relationship of significance in family functioning.

Check *not applicable* where above are not present.

INADEQUATE	MARGINAL	ADEQUATE
Separated partner does not support when so ordered, or is extremely disturbing influence on family.	Separated partner does not support adequately or regularly or is a disturbing influence in family.	Couple lives together.
Extramarital relations are endangering children's welfare, or have come to attention of law.	Extramarital relations exist but do not openly affect welfare of children.	Extramarital relations, if present at all, are minimal and transitory, and have not been allowed to jeopardize family solidarity.
Emotional tie is so deficient that children are endangered.	Weak emotional tie between partners, lack of concern for each other.	Positive emotional tie between partners who can express need for the other's help and respond appropriately to need. Considerable pleasure derived from shared experiences.

INADEQUATE	MARGINAL	ADEQUATE
Severe, persistent marital conflict, necessitating intervention by authorities or threatening complete disruption of family life.	There are some points of agreement between parents, but disagreement and conflict tend to predominate and obscure them.	Consistent effort to limit scope and duration of marital conflict and keep communication open for resolution of conflicts which arise.

2. Parent-Child Relationship

INADEQUATE	MARGINAL	ADEQUATE
No affection is shown between parents and children. Great indifference or marked rejection of children. No respect shown for one another. No approval, recognition or encouragement shown to children. If any concern shown at all by parents, it takes the form of rank discrimination in favor of a few against the rest. Parent-Child conflict extremely severe. (Above so serious as to constitute neglect as legally defined, and warrant intervention by authorities.)	Affection between parents and children is intermittent, or weak, or obscured by conflict. Parents' anger unpredictable and unrelated to specific conduct of children. Family members played off against each other. Marked favoritism with no attempt to compensate disadvantaged children. Little mutual respect or concern for each other. Parents and children frequently in conflict. (Above present, but danger to children is potential—not actual.)	Affection is shown between parents and children. Parents try always to be consistent in treatment of children. Children have sense of belonging, emotional security. Children and parents show respect for each other, mutual concern. Parent-child conflict is minimal or restricted by consistent attention, free communication, and desire for harmony.

3. Relationship Among Children

INADEQUATE	MARGINAL	ADEQUATE
Conflict between children resulting in physical violence or	Emotional ties among children are weak. Rarely play together.	Positive emotional ties and mutual identification among

INADEQUATE	MARGINAL	ADEQUATE
cruelty which warrants intervention.	Fighting occurs often, teasing, bullying, other emotional or physical cruelty. Children rarely share playthings, show little loyalty to one another or pride in other's achievements.	children. Depending on age, often play together, share their playthings. Loyal to each other, enjoy other's company, take pride in achievements of their siblings. Fighting and bickering normal for age.

4. *Family Solidarity*

INADEQUATE	MARGINAL	ADEQUATE
Marked lack of affection and emotional ties among family members. Conflict among members persistent or severe.	Little emotional warmth is evidenced among family members. Family members often in conflict.	Warmth and affection are shown among family members, giving them a sense of belonging and emotional security. Conflict within family dealt with quickly and appropriately.
Marked lack of cohesiveness and mutual concern, satisfactions in family living not evident. No pride in family or sense of family identity. Members plan on basis personal gratification rather than family as whole. Serious danger of family disruption. (Above so serious that laws relating to neglect or cruelty violated or family	Little cohesiveness, such as members rarely doing things together, eating together; little planning toward common family goals; little feeling of collective responsibility; little pulling together in crisis. Few satisfactions in family living. (Above presents potential but not yet actual danger to welfare of children.) Family's solidarity	Definite evidence of cohesiveness: *e.g.*, members often do things together; eat together; family plans and works toward some common goals; definite feeling of collective responsibility; members pull together in times of stress. Members find considerable satisfaction in family living. Cohesiveness not at odds with the welfare of the community.

INADEQUATE	MARGINAL	ADEQUATE
welfare so threatened that intervention justified.)	assumes antisocial forms.	

B. *Individual Behavior and Adjustment*

1. *Individual Behavior of Parents*

Check separately for mother and father. Check "not applicable" if parent has no tie to family (as indicated under marital relationship). If there are more than one mother or father figures with ties to family, check the one who has the strongest tie with the family. Check "inadequate" if consequences of law violations (incarceration, probation, etc.) are still operative; however, prolonged probation should be weighed with other factors.

INADEQUATE	MARGINAL	ADEQUATE
Socially Delinquent Behavior:	*Socially Delinquent Behavior:*	*Socially Delinquent Behavior:*
Is incarcerated or on probation for law violation. Seriously deviant sexual behavior (promiscuity, etc.) or serious offenses against family (assault, incest, etc.) endangering welfare of children. Excessive drinking severely affecting family welfare (reducing budget below minimal level, causing severe conflict, etc.) and warranting intervention for sake of children.	Minor law violations not resulting in incarceration or probation, deviant sexual conduct, offenses against family, or excessive drinking, but not seriously affecting family welfare. Deficiency in social skills which handicaps comfortable relationships to people and institutions.	Law violations are limited to such slight infractions as minor traffic violations. Drinking or extramarital relations not a serious problem to individual or to family. Has fair complement of social skills, relates comfortably to most people and institutions.
Mental-Physical State:	*Mental-Physical State:*	*Mental-Physical State:*
Serious mental illness requiring interven-	Mental or emotional disorder is present	Mental health is good. Psychosocial

INADEQUATE	MARGINAL	ADEQUATE
tion or resulting in institutionalization.	but able to function on minimal level, not actually dangerous to family.	functioning at the level of individual's potential.
Mental defectiveness requiring institutionalization or so limiting capacity to maintain family life that special help or training necessary.	Mental retardation seriously limiting functioning.	Performs up to mental capacity and able to function adequately in most areas.
Parent has disease which endangers public health, has not sought or carried through on treatment, health authorities have right to intervene, chronic or major physical disease or handicap so disabling that person unable to provide the minimum care for children who are his major responsibility.	Chronic or major physical disease or handicap which is somewhat disabling, but permits minimal functioning especially in regard to care of children.	Diseases or handicaps not of serious nature, receiving appropriate treatment, functioning hampered only slightly if at all.

Role Performance [1]

As Spouse: If deserted or separated, does not support when so ordered. Extramarital liaisons endangering family. Severe conflict with

Role Performance [1]

As Spouse: Frequent conflict or disagreement with spouse in many areas of living, emotional tie weak.

Role Performance [1]

As Spouse: Conflict with spouse is minimal, dealt with appropriately; extramarital affairs rare, positive emotional tie, disagreements

---

[1] Due allowance should be made for variations in parental roles made necessary by the particular family structure. Thus the mother's role as supplementary or chief wage earner needs to be considered where children do not have to be looked after during the day. The father's role as homemaker may have to be reviewed where he is unable to earn a living, etc.

INADEQUATE	MARGINAL	ADEQUATE
spouse damaging to children.		well handled or well tolerated.
As Parent: Violation of laws relating to neglect of children, assault, incest, etc., making intervention necessary.	*As Parent:* Little concern for or interest in children. Displays little affection for them, physical and emotional care provided minimal. Shows favoritism.	*As Parent:* Positive relationship with children, shows them affection, spends time with them, provides appropriate physical and emotional care.
As Breadwinner: If absent, does not support when so ordered. If at home, and physically able to work, is unable or unwilling to support family.	*As Breadwinner:* Provides marginal or uncertain income, but little or no PA required. (Unless so disabled as to require outside support.)	*As Breadwinner:* Provides income for family enabling above-minimal living standard. Works regularly at full-time job, has positive feeling for job.
As Homemaker: Housekeeping and care of children so inadequate that it constitutes neglect and warrants intervention.	*As Homemaker:* Housekeeping and care of children poor, but health of family not seriously endangered.	*As Homemaker:* Housekeeping and care of children is generally good.
As Member of Community: Law violations other than offenses against family. Extremely hostile attitude toward community—children encouraged to commit antisocial acts.	*As Member of Community:* Has little or no social contacts with neighbors, relatives, etc., belongs to no social groups, is dissatisfied with social status. Has a generally hostile attitude toward community, makes poor use of resources.	*As Member of Community:* Has meaningful ties with friends, relatives, etc. Belongs to some social groups which provide satisfactions, is comfortable with social status, with or without some desire to improve it. Has positive attitude toward community, makes good use of

INADEQUATE	MARGINAL	ADEQUATE
		facilities when necessary.

2. *Individual Behavior and Adjustment of Children*

For purposes of scoring, children 10 and over are considered together, as are children from 1 to 9. The total score for each group is determined by finding the average of separate scores. Do not consider children who are *permanently* out of home.

INADEQUATE	MARGINAL	ADEQUATE
Acting Out Behavior:	*Acting Out Behavior:*	*Acting Out Behavior:*
Acting out, disruptive, antisocial behavior of serious concern and indicative of a child in real danger, warranting intervention. Incarcerated or on probation.	Acting out, disruptive, antisocial behavior of less serious nature, not a long-standing pattern, not indicative of more serious problems, therefore intervention not warranted.	Acting out behavior is normal for age— pranks, mischievousness, etc., not of serious nature.
Mental-Physical State:	*Mental-Physical State:*	*Mental-Physical State:*
Mental illness requiring intervention or resulting in hospitalization. Excessively withdrawn or other behavior suggesting emotional disturbance or serious problems in relating to others.	Emotional disorder evident, but receiving treatment or not serious enough to justify intervention.	Emotional health appears good, enjoys appropriate activities, relates well to others.
Mental defectiveness requiring institutional training or custodial care that is not provided.	Performance below mental and/or physical capacity. Mental retardation severely limiting functioning, but special training, such as special class received.	Performs up to mental and physical capacity and able to function adequately in most areas.

INADEQUATE	MARGINAL	ADEQUATE
Child has disease which endangers public health, no measures taken for isolation or treatment. Other serious health conditions or handicaps for which proper care is not provided.	Child not retarded, but performs well below capacity. Presence of chronic or major physical disease or handicap receiving some treatment, but permits minimal functioning.	Diseases or handicaps if present are receiving appropriate care with resulting favorable adjustment.

Role Performance	*Role Performance*	*Role Performance*
As Child: Violent destructive, or assaultive behavior against family members.	*As Child:* Gets along poorly with parents and siblings, rarely performs household duties.	*As Child:* Close ties to family members. Continuous participation in household duties and family life.
As Pupil: Excessive truancy, disruptiveness, incorrigibility, property destruction causing intervention. Other infringements of school regulations resulting in suspension, expulsion, etc.	*As Pupil:* Acting out or withdrawn behavior of less serious nature. Attendance not regular but no action taken. School work poor. Little positive feeling toward school.	*As Pupil:* Attends regularly, school work approximates ability, positive attitude toward school. Acting out limited to occasional pranks.
As Member of Peer Groups: Participation with others in delinquent acts. So unable to relate to peers as to be severely disturbed emotionally. Often involved in severe conflicts with peers.	*As Member of Peer Groups:* Has few friends, belongs to no peer groups, conflict with peers common.	*As Member of Peer Groups:* Is well liked, has friends, belongs to one or more peer groups.

C. *Care and Training of Children*

1. *Physical Care*

INADEQUATE	MARGINAL	ADEQUATE
Supply and care of clothes, cleanliness, diet, and health care provided for children seriously endangers their health or threatens adjustment in school and acceptance in peer groups. Vermin a serious health or social handicap. (Above so serious that intervention warranted.)	Children have few clothes, which are dirty and not mended, pay little attention to cleanliness, receive unbalanced, unnutritious diet. Parents lax in looking after health needs of children, but health of children and social adjustment are not threatened to the extent that intervention is justified.	Children have suitable clothes, are kept clean, diet well balanced and wholesome, health needs are looked after promptly.

2. *Training Methods and Emotional Care*

INADEQUATE	MARGINAL	ADEQUATE
Affection is rarely shown to children, marked indifference or obvious rejection. Parents have pathological tie to children, use them as pawns. Physical and emotional cruelty. (Above so serious that intervention is warranted.)	Little affection is shown to children, parents usually indifferent to or reject children, or are overpermissive. Children have little sense of emotional security. (Above potential rather than actual danger to children.)	Parents show steady affection for children, provide atmosphere of emotional warmth, sense of belonging.
Parents' behavior standards are so deviant from wider community that children are encouraged	Parents' behavior standards in many respects somewhat deviant from community, or there is a	Parents' ideas of how children should behave are generally those acceptable to community. Stand-

INADEQUATE	MARGINAL	ADEQUATE
toward antisocial acts.	lack of standards, or parents expect too much or too little maturity.	ards of behavior are appropriate to age level.
Physical punishment overly severe, or inappropriate. Extreme lack of discipline. Inconsistency of methods in one parent or between parents, limits not enforced, strong disagreement between parents on training. Approval shown rarely or not at all. (Above directly contributes to delinquent behavior or otherwise puts children in danger.)	Parents are overly rigid, overpermissive, indifferent. Physical punishment, swearing occurs. Discipline not appropriate to behavior. Approval of good conduct rare. Parents are inconsistent, often do not enforce limits, disagree with each other over exercise of discipline, do not share task of training. Parents show favoritism. (Above potential rather than actual danger.)	Parents are neither overly rigid nor overly permissive, physical punishment rare. Method used usually appropriate to behavior. Approval of good conduct often shown. Parents are fairly consistent in exercising discipline, enforce limits set, agree with each other in exercising discipline, share job of training children.

D. *Social Activities*

1. *Informal Associations*

INADEQUATE	MARGINAL	ADEQUATE
Conflict with relatives, neighbors, friends resulting in physical violence or illegal activities. Persons as above such a disturbing and discordant influence on family as to endanger welfare of children. Participation with friends in	Broken, discordant, indifferent relationships to relatives. Frequent squabbles with neighbors. Family members have few or no social outlets with friends or have friends whose influence leads to dubious social consequences (drunken	Majority of relationships with relatives are pleasant and satisfying. Fairly amicable relationships maintained with neighbors. Family members have social outlets with friends providing recreational and interpersonal satisfactions,

INADEQUATE	MARGINAL	ADEQUATE
perpetrating delin- quent antisocial acts.	sprees, destruction of property, children left alone, etc.)	sense of identification with larger groups, provide necessary socialization experi- ences for children.

2. *Formal Associations*

INADEQUATE	MARGINAL	ADEQUATE
Membership in formal groups per- petrating antisocial acts. Behavior in organized group so destructive or disrup- tive that intervention is necessary.	Family members be- long to no organized groups. No activity with groups having a civic orientation. Family feels socially rejected and unable to improve social status.	Family members, where appropriate, belong to some clubs, organizations, unions, etc. Some members active in groups which lend support to commu- nity betterment.

E. *Economic Practices*
1. *Source and Amount of Income*

INADEQUATE	MARGINAL	ADEQUATE
Income entirely from general relief because of failure of able- bodied head of household to support (except temporary layoffs, and ADC or other payments due to absence or hus- band or his disabil- ity). Income from PA obtained through fraudulent means. Income derived from theft, forgery, etc.	Income derived part- ly from general relief because head of household unable to hold a steady job or laid off because of employment situa- tion, unless disabled, because of physical handicap, mental ill- ness or deficiency. Children of working age who are not in school, service, etc., are not working.	Income derived from work of family mem- bers, or from sources such as pensions, rent, support pay- ments, etc., but money is not from public funds (except for pensions, A.D.C., A.B., O.A.A. etc.).
Amount of income so low or unstable that basic necessities not provided for children.	Amount of income marginal or unstable, barely meets family needs.	Family sufficiently independent finan- cially to afford a few luxuries or savings, is fairly well satisfied

INADEQUATE	MARGINAL	ADEQUATE
		with economic status, and working toward greater financial security.

2. *Job Situation*

INADEQUATE	MARGINAL	ADEQUATE
Behavior on job breaks the law, as fraud, embezzlement, robbery, physical violence to coworkers. Able-bodied man unwilling to obtain employment.	Frequent changes of job, unsteady work pattern, works less than full time, job is below capacity. Poor relations with boss and coworkers, dissatisfied with job.	Works regularly at full time job, seeks advancement, changes jobs only when unavoidable due to economic or other circumstances, or for improvement. Job is suitable for person's capabilities, maintains harmonious relations with boss and coworkers, has positive feeling toward job.

3. *Use of Money*

INADEQUATE	MARGINAL	ADEQUATE
Severe conflict over control of income endangering children's welfare. Budgeting and money management so poor that basic necessities not provided. Excessive debt resulting in garnishment, or reduces family budget as above.	Disagreement over control of income leading to conflict among family members. Family unable to live within budget, money management poor, luxuries take precedence over basic necessities, impulsive spending. (Above not seriously endangering children's welfare.)	Money spent on basis of agreement that such is responsibility of one or more members of family. Family budgets income, money management carried out with realistic regard to basic necessities. Debts are relatively few, and seldom incurred for luxuries; they are manageable and planned for in budget.

NOTE: Above applies only to family members contributing substantially to support of family.

F. *Household Practices*

1. *Physical Facilities*

INADEQUATE	MARGINAL	ADEQUATE
Property is so deteriorated, kept in such poor state of repair, facilities for sleeping, washing, sanitation, heat, water, refrigeration, or cooking so inadequate as to be an actual threat to the physical and emotional welfare of family members, particularly children; situation necessitates intervention by health or other authorities.	Property is deteriorated, in poor state of repair, sufficient space not available. Absence or inadequacy of basic household equipment. (Above potentially harmful to welfare of children.)	Property is kept in good condition, sufficient space for family members. Necessary household equipment available and in good working order.

2. *Housekeeping Standards*

INADEQUATE	MARGINAL	ADEQUATE
Home is maintained in such a dirty and unsanitary condition, meals so irregular, diet so inadequate as to constitute an actual hazard to physical well-being of children. Vermin or rats present serious health hazard.	Home is in disorder, meals irregular, diet poorly planned, making a potential hazard to physical welfare of children.	Home is maintained in a condition conducive to good health, hygiene, and a sense of orderliness. Meals served regularly, diet is well balanced and nutritious. Attention paid to making home attractive.

G. *Health Conditions and Practices*

1. *Health Problems*

INADEQUATE	MARGINAL	ADEQUATE
Presence of communicable disease en-	Presence of disease, major chronic illness	Physical health of family members is

INADEQUATE	MARGINAL	ADEQUATE
dangering public health, not isolated or properly treated. Major or chronic disease or handicap so severely limiting person's functioning within and without the home that there is an actual threat to family welfare, particularly the care children are receiving.	or handicaps which limits person's functioning inside and outside home, but constitutes no actual threat to family welfare.	such that they are able to function adequately in their various roles.
Proper treatment or quarantine not secured for diseases endangering life of person and/or public health. Parents neglect or refuse to provide medical or other remedial care for health and well-being of children. Disease prevention practices (sanitation, diet, etc.) not followed. Conditions so poor that physical neglect of children is involved.	Refusal or failure to get or continue medical care other than in column to left. Medical instructions disregarded or not followed consistently. Disease prevention practices not generally followed, but health of children not seriously endangered.	Concern is shown about ill health or handicaps, medical care promptly sought when needed, medical instructions followed. Disease prevention practices are observed.

H. *Relationship to Family Centered Worker*

1. *Attitude Toward Worker*

INADEQUATE	MARGINAL	ADEQUATE
Physical violence or verbal assault and other types of insult-	Worker met with hostility, resentment, or defensiveness on	Worker is received with friendliness and readiness to consider

NOTE: Mental illness is *not* to be considered here, but is evaluated under Individual Behavior and Adjustment.

INADEQUATE	MARGINAL	ADEQUATE
ing behavior.	part of family; or marked indifference shown.	family problems in relation to services offered.

2. *Use of Worker*

INADEQUATE	MARGINAL	ADEQUATE
Refusal to talk with worker when the basis of community concern is such that the worker has a right to stay in the situation. Absolute refusal to acknowledge any problems.	Apathy apparent in dealing with caseworker. Reluctance shown to recognize and/or deal with major family problems.	Willingness is shown to work together with worker on major problems facing the family. Awareness shown of the major problems upon which casework has been concentrating and effort made to work toward solution of problem.

I. *Use of Community Resources*
1. *School*

INADEQUATE	MARGINAL	ADEQUATE
Parents are extremely hostile to school, encourage or abet consistent truancy, are antagonistic to school personnel; refuse co-operation when this is necessary due to seriousness of community concern.	Parents place little value on education, take little interest in children's school activities, are lax in enforcing attendance, are unco-operative with school in plans for children.	Parents value education for their children, see that they attend school regularly, are co-operative with school personnel when joint planning is indicated.
Children have extremely negative attitude toward school, are excessively truant without excuse, are	Children have negative attitude toward school, truant rather frequently, are disruptive or a disturb-	Children like school, attend regularly, are not behavior problems, achieve according to capacity.

INADEQUATE	MARGINAL	ADEQUATE
very disruptive, destroy school property, commit other infringements of school regulations demanding intervention.	ing influence; do poor school work, but not sufficiently serious to warrant intervention.	

2. *Church*

INADEQUATE	MARGINAL	ADEQUATE
Law violations directed against church, as robbery, destruction of property, committing nuisances, vandalism, etc. Instilling hostile attitudes in children toward religion. Serious religious conflict between parents has negative effect upon children.	Using church for purposes sharply at variance with aims of church, as being an extremely disruptive influence in a church group. Children are permitted to attend Sunday School or church social activities, but parents oppose or show negative attitudes toward church.	Attend church fairly regularly, derive personal satisfaction from church tie.

3. *Health Resources*

(including mental health)

INADEQUATE	MARGINAL	ADEQUATE
Hostility or bitterness or apathy toward available health resources so great that serious health problems of children do	Family regards health resources with suspicion, hostility, resentment. Agencies used unconstructively, appointments	Family has positive attitude toward health agencies, available facilities are used promptly when need arises,

NOTE: Check under "Marginal" and "Adequate" only if family member(s) are *active* members of a church or church group. If there are no church ties, or only nominal church membership, check "not appropriate." "Inadequate" applies whether or not there are church ties.

INADEQUATE	MARGINAL	ADEQUATE
not receive medical care, or health needs of parents that prevent them from caring for children are not met.	are missed, follow-through lacking, medical advice not followed, but not to extent of seriously endangering children's welfare.	appointments are kept, medical advice followed.

4. *Social Agencies*

(includes probation, housing authority, employment agencies, etc. as well as casework agencies.)

INADEQUATE	MARGINAL	ADEQUATE
Extreme hostility to social agencies leading to behavior such as assault, robbery, or destruction of property, fraud, etc. Refusal to accept agency services where this has been ordered by law or is necessary because of community concern about children.	Attitude toward agencies marked by hostility, resentment, defensiveness, apathy, etc. Agencies used unconstructively—family is not co-operative, or is apathetic, or overly demanding, etc.	Attitude toward agencies is positive. Family utilizes agencies appropriately for improvement of family life or for meeting needs of individual members. Show co-operation in working on joint plans.

5. *Recreational Agencies*

INADEQUATE	MARGINAL	ADEQUATE
Hostility toward recreational agencies leads to assault, robbery, destruction of property, etc. Parents prevent children from using organized recreational facilities.	Children seldom use organized recreational groups—such as playgrounds. If use is made, behavior is characterized by disruptiveness, nonco-operation, etc.	Family members, particularly children, make use of available recreational resources according to age and interest which provide satisfaction and necessary socialization experience (for children).

INDEX

(Capital letters used for categories of family functioning)

223